ADVANCE IN LIFE

FROM REVELATION
TO INSPIRATION
TO MANIFESTATION

JESSE DUPLANTIS

Tulsa, OK

ADVANCE IN LIFE
From Revelation to Inspiration to Manifestation
ISBN: 978-1-68031-232-4

Copyright © 2018 Jesse Duplantis
Jesse Duplantis Ministries, Destrehan, LA 70047
www.jdm.org

Published by Harrison House Publishers
Tulsa, Oklahoma 74145
www.harrisonhouse.com

Contents

Introduction

One day I was praying and talking to God about what He would have me speak about for the New Year. I always do this at the end of one year in preparation for the next, just in case God has something He wants me to share as a theme. The Lord doesn't always give me a theme; each year is different. But, sometimes, He gives me a message that isn't just for one particular year but is a message for life.

As I prayed, the Lord spoke to my heart and asked me a question: "If you could define Christianity in one word, what would it be?"

I said, "What did You say?" He said, "If you could take Christianity and define it, and put it into one word, what would it be?"

So, I started thinking about it. I thought, *Power.* Then, I thought, *No, it is Healing or Grace.* Then, of course, I finally thought, *Salvation.* The Lord answered me in my spirit, "No, it's ADVANCE."

I immediately thought of my ministry and told Him, "I thought we've already been doing that." He said, "You haven't seen anything yet." Right then, revelation began to flow through me—but not just for my own life and ministry. The Lord began to flood my mind with the implications of that word and how it applies to the life of a believer, and ultimately Christianity as a result.

ADVANCE. I began to preach on it exclusively. I began to write my Partners and friends with teaching to inspire them to do it. Out of that, this book was born. I realized at the moment God spoke that word that everything—and I do mean everything—God is and does in the lives of His children moves *forward.* So, Christianity itself must always be moving forward too because that is what God intended believers to do. It's what He created humanity to do.

We aren't meant to back up. We aren't meant to give up. We have always been meant to advance. This book is not about prayer,

1

although prayer should be a part of the believer's everyday life—this is a book about manifesting what God has put on your heart. It's about creating a mindset to advance. It's about letting go of the limitations we put on ourselves and reaching forward to all God has for us, so that while we are advancing personally, we are also advancing Christianity as a whole.

The Lord showed me that if we will align ourselves with Him and do things His way, we can and will advance more quickly than we ever have before. I hope that this book will cause you to seek God about it—to get a revelation that produces inspiration, so that you see manifestation in your own life.

We can manifest our own true desires. We can manifest His desires too and move Christianity forward—because that's what He wants. God wants the whole world to be given the opportunity to know Him. The message of salvation and the principles of the Word are so very important to God's plan.

In this book I am going to share many different thoughts, principles, and warnings that have helped me to see God's plan come to pass in my own life. I'm going to share some of my thoughts on some current problems I see in the Church and in society, too. I pray that you will glean some wisdom for your own life so that you move forward in doing and having what God has put on your heart.

I really believe that this is your time. Adventures with God are just around the corner if you have the audacity to run your race in faith. Your true desires and the vision that God has placed in your heart is important, and there is no better time than now to believe.

So, I want to encourage you. Now. Today. It's time to do what the apostle Paul said. It's time to forget what's behind you. It's time to reach out for what is before you. This is your time to press toward your mark and ***ADVANCE***.

CHAPTER 1

ADVANCE!
Aim to Advance in ALL Areas

God didn't design us for "one-sided" advancement—we were created to advance in all areas. Health matters. Finances matter. Relationships matter. Personal goals, dreams, and visions matter. God's plan for the world matters, too.

The great limitation that most people have in life is thinking that they have to pick one area to focus on—as if they don't have energy, faith, or power to advance in more than one area at a time. Wrong.

Sure, you may have one area that needs more attention because it's been on the backburner, but you can advance much more fully than you might be giving yourself credit for because God lives in you—that makes you more than powerful. Don't let anybody lie to you! You can do all things through Christ who gives you strength and you have enough faith to move mountains! (Philippians 4:13; Mark 11:23)

Now, I know that some believers focus only on advancing spiritually, but God wouldn't have given us a body, and a desire for relationships, and put us in an economic world if we didn't need full-circle advancement in our lives.

When You Only Focus on the Physical

Have you ever seen a top athlete? An Olympian? A man or woman in tip-top physical shape? Most people who advance to that level in their body have had to overcome a lot in their mind. I know. I've met quite a few. Some, who are believers, have realized their need for God and built up their spirit, too.

But what happens to a person who is *only* advancing physically? Well, they may create a physical body that is working at peak level. They become specimens of great health and fitness that everybody admires. But inside? Their spirit is atrophied and looks frail—it's crying out for advancement. If they don't tend to themselves, their heart will gnaw at them to meet that need, but because they have no knowledge of what the need really is, they'll sabotage themselves.

How many people climb to the top athletic echelons and then destroy themselves in other ways and ruin their career? Many have done just that. Why? Because physical exertion, no matter how many endorphins are kicked up and flying, can't burn away the mind's need for peace and the spirit's need for God. In other words, physical advancement alone can't satisfy—and that means whether you obtain perfect outward beauty or perfect internal health, physical advancement shouldn't be the only area of advancement in your life.

My joke is that it doesn't matter how healthy you are—if you don't have any money, you aren't going anywhere! And I don't care how good you look—if you don't treat people in your life right, you won't have anybody to go anywhere with! You can't only focus on the physical. God made you, and you are more than just a body.

4

When You Only Focus on Finances

Now, some people focus only on making money, and they may accomplish great things and generate millions or even billions in the world. They may revolutionize an entire industry. They may build a business worth a fortune. Some may even change the way the world works, in one way or another. As a result, they may accumulate a lot of finances in life.

Financial advancement might look like the pinnacle of ALL advancement, but it's not. If it's your *only* focus, you are not advancing in the way God designed you to advance. How many rich miserable people are there out there? You'd be surprised! Many. If money alone solved the problem of peace, security, and joy, all rich people would be happy all the time. They'd be fulfilled by their power to purchase. They aren't. Because you cannot ignore the spirit or the body at the expense of making money and be happy for long.

Now, let me say this: I've been rich and I've been poor—and rich is better! It can't make you happy, but it sure can make you more comfortable in your misery! The truth is that no matter how enjoyable it may be to reach financial goals, it's impossible for riches or wealth to meet human spiritual needs. Physical "things" can't solve spiritual problems.

The real and point-blank-blunt eventuality about this life is this: Nobody's getting out of here alive! You know it. I know it. It's the way it is. So, finances definitely matter, but they aren't the only thing that matters because of this verse: *"For what shall it profit a man, if he shall gain the whole world, and lose his own soul?"* (Mark 8:36). Spiritual advancement trumps it all in the end. We will all be held accountable to God one day.

Now, out of all of the ways we can advance, financial advancement seems to drive *some* people to really lose sight of their need for advancement in other areas. They may work themselves at the expense of their body and their spirit, and even to the detriment of their closest relationships.

So, the joke flips around this way: It doesn't matter how much money you have—if you are as sick as a dog, you aren't going anywhere! And no matter how rich you get—if you don't treat your spouse and kids right, you're going to be one miserable person in the end. They'll make sure of it!

When You Only Focus on Relationships

Relationships! They are the most valuable things in life. But, if you choose to *only* focus on your earthly relationships, you will lose out in one way or another. Think about it: How many wonderful mothers and fathers didn't take care of their bodies and went to an early grave? How many lived in constant pressure and stress of having enough finances? And how many couples today, right this moment, are trying to make peace with each other—when what they really need to do is make peace with God and themselves?

Let me tell you something (and this is no joke!), without health, you won't enjoy your relationships for long, no matter how good they are. Without finances, the stress of lack will steal your energy and drain the joy out of your relationships. There is a reason why problems surrounding finances are so often mentioned when people divorce. And lastly, without spiritual advancement, you cannot really know how to love yourself or others God's way, which is the best way. It's hard to experience good relationships with others when you aren't even at peace with yourself!

As my daughter says, "How can you 'Do unto others as you would have them do unto you' if you don't know how to 'do unto YOU'?" In other words, how are you going to know how to treat others if you don't know how to treat yourself? And how will you know how to treat yourself with love if you don't know the One Who is defined as "Love"?—God!

The greatest relationship you will ever have is the one between you and God. It's the pinnacle because it's the foundation—and our faith in God for everything we want or need is born out of our faith in His love for us.

You cannot really build the kind of relationships you want with others unless you (1) allow God into your life so you can connect with His powerful love, (2) see yourself through that love so you can find peace with yourself, and (3) let His love start flowing out of your heart into the lives of others so that you can have peace with others.

God sent His only begotten Son to die for you—because He valued you that much. He gave His best because He thought you were worth it. Do you think you are worth it? Let me tell you something. When you find God's love, you find *your* value. When you find your value, you will suddenly find a lot more value for *others*. And when you value others, you won't be so tempted to treat them like used up and worthless trash.

You don't hurt or cut down what you cherish. You don't disrespect, use, or abuse what you value and love. If you want to read what the God kind of love really looks like, go to 1 Corinthians 13 and get yourself a revelation—and let that revelation turn into inspiration. It's the only way you'll get to the point of manifestation. And if you want to manifest anything, I promise you want to manifest the love of God because that's the nature of God, and the ripple effects of His kind of love are life-changing.

Spiritual advancement is the foundation of ALL advancement for a reason—but nothing happens if you don't take action. The love of God is always extended to you, but it's up to you to accept it and start learning about it so that you can really know it and flow in it on a regular basis.

The Goal of Christianity Is to Advance

The Gospel is God's message of salvation through Jesus Christ's birth, death, and resurrection—and it's a message for all of mankind. Redemption is available to everyone. As believers, it's our blessing to share what we've been given.

My life is about fulfilling the Great Commission to *"Go ye into all the world, and preach the Gospel to every creature"* (Mark 16:15). It's a mission I don't take lightly, but like every other minister with that calling, we cannot do it alone—we need everyone doing his or her part to reach people and change lives, one soul at a time.

There are people I will never be able to reach, but you may be able to reach them. We all have a destiny, and part of our destiny is affecting others for good—and there is no better "good" than helping others to be free spiritually because that freedom unlocks the opportunity to be free in every other area. God cares about the whole person, not just one area of their lives, and we are His hands and feet on the earth. This means that your personal advancement is intricately woven into the advancement of Christianity as a whole.

You see, we aren't meant to live only for ourselves—that is what people without God do, and it's a very one-sided and selfish adventure. To advance God's way is to advance in our own personal lives as well as in the lives of others. That's His plan. So that should be our plan, too. It's God's will that we are generous with what we've been given and affect others for good by sharing His message in His way.

Every word you say to help others find God and find freedom in any area of their life is a seed that God sees. Every action you take in the life of another is important to Him. You may see the results here or you may only see the results once you get to Heaven; it really doesn't matter. One day in Heaven, you *will* know the fullness of all your seeds into the lives of others. Until then, just know that God keeps the books. He knows it all and sees—and one day, you will too. Just do your part knowing that you are a part of something big!

Real Christianity is open, pure, and joyful. It's called "Good News" for a reason! It's motivated by an honest desire for what is good in life—good for us, good for others, and good for the whole world. *"For God so loved the world, that He gave His only begotten Son, that whosoever believeth in Him should not perish, but have everlasting life"* (John 3:16).

"Everlasting life" doesn't start when we die; it begins the moment we receive Christ and reconnect with God as our Father, the Creator and Source of it all—that's when our spiritual advancement begins, and from that moment on, we are meant to start advancing in this life. Heaven awaits us as believers, but this life counts, too. Spiritually, physically, financially, or in our relationships with other people, God sent His Son to give us life—and not just any old, boring life.

Jesus said it best when He revealed His own purpose for coming to the world: *"The thief cometh not, but for to steal, and to kill, and to destroy: I am come that they might have life, and that they might have it more abundantly"* (John 10:10). Advancing in life is God's will, and it's available to any believer who has the audacity to believe.

ADVANCE IN LIFE

CHAPTER 2

Forget What's Behind, Press Forward to What's Ahead

The scriptural text I enjoy most on advancement was written by the apostle Paul to the church at Philippi. I like it so much that I have it framed and outside my office door so that I see it every single day.

...But this one thing I do, forgetting those things which are behind, and reaching forth unto those things which are before,

I press toward the mark for the prize of the high calling of God in Christ Jesus.

Philippians 3:13-14

I like how Paul says "this one thing I do," because just in that one statement, he is drilling down to the nuts and bolts of his everyday life. This is his focus. This is what he chooses every day. Paul chooses to forget the things of the past—whatever happened, happened, and he cannot go back and do anything about those things. He knows this and yet refuses to get caught in the mental trap of rehearsing the past. What an amazing revelation just in that little bit of the verse.

It doesn't matter if what happened in the past was great or terrible—it is now gone, done, and over. You cannot go back, no matter how much you think about it, and change it or relive it in real time. Paul is not talking about the enjoyment of having memories. He's talking about reaching his destiny and using forward-motion-thinking as an everyday discipline in order to advance in his faith in God's plan.

So, why are so many people talking about negative stuff that happened yesterday, last year, or maybe even fifty years ago? You know, I had a great day yesterday—I decided to let it go. Why? Because I'm never going to be able to relive it. I allow myself the memory, but I do not allow myself to make that memory the focus of today. Today is for today. So I'm thinking about today! And I'm looking forward to what I can do today, and how that will pave the way for tomorrow. I have goals and dreams, of course, so I have to look ahead.

My Mother Isn't in My Past—She's in My Future
Death Loses Its Sting Each Time I Press Forward
to What Lies Ahead

Even death loses its sting when you look forward instead of backward. For instance, I lost my mother on Easter Sunday in 1982. Now, every Easter I cannot help but think of her and remember on that day. But to only think of the past would steal the joy from the present day—in fact, I could completely ruin the day for myself and lose the joy of spending time with my grandchild in the present if I were to dwell only on the past when it comes to my mother. So, I don't do that. I honor my mother and remember her, but I know that in order to move forward, I must forget those things which are behind to a degree, and press forward to what lies ahead in Christ Jesus.

So, I made a choice a long time ago and that choice is this: My mother's death is behind me. Does that sound hard and callous? It's not. For me, this is about pressing forward in hope. It's about changing my perspective from the past to the future. What's in the future? Reunion! Her earthly death is behind me because her eternity in Heaven is in front of me. I press forward knowing the truth, which is this: She's not in my past; she's in my future!

I will see her again because my mother is in my future. That is the great and wonderful hope I have in Christ. That's what I press toward on Easter Sunday each year, or any day that I think of her and feel those feelings. I miss her, sure! But I know she's in my future. I have something to look forward to when it comes to my mother. We all do when it comes to our loved ones who pass to Heaven before we do. They aren't in our past. They are in our future! Because I'm pressing forward to the good that lies ahead, I can allow myself to forget those things which are behind.

You see, the only thing that died was my mother's body—but she is alive and well today, right now. Mama always liked a party and she chose to go out on Resurrection Sunday, the most glorious day for Christians. One thing that always helps me feel good is just thinking that, when I see her, she won't be sick or old. She will be young! I'll get to see my mama like my daddy saw her when she was young and beaming with health. My dad met her when she was 15 years old, and that's what I'm going to see when we meet up again in Heaven. Imagine that! I can hardly wait to see her like that!

I have so many family members who have gone on to be with Jesus—and not one of them is in my past. All are in my future. Thinking that way gives me a wonderful hope. It's salve for the soul and even brings excitement. I mean, can you imagine seeing your great-grandfather as a young and healthy man?

Whoever you loved who has gone onto Heaven is not "lost." Do you know what really happened? They moved! If you could compare death to punctuation, death would be a comma—a pause before you keep on going. Remember, the real person is never just the body— the real person is the combination of the spirit and soul. They live forever, like it or not! And a glorious reunion is coming.

Do you see how shifting your perspective to what lies ahead can even change one of the hardest things, like remembering the death of a loved one? You choose the thoughts you allow to be rehearsed in your head. Any thought can arise, but choosing to shift your thought forward to the truth will always help you.

So, if you have the option, why not choose what is good? Why not choose what is true? Why not choose what brings you hope and even joy? It's so much better to choose thoughts based on God's holy Word! Heaven is real and it's a blessed hope, but while you are still on earth, your life must continue to advance. God is with you and your departed loved ones are in your future, not your past. Do not forget it!

There Is a Mark and a Prize IN Christ Jesus— To Advance You Must Be Reaching Out and Pressing Toward Your Mark

I like the way Paul says in Philippians 3:13-14 that he is "reaching forth" to what is before him, because it illustrates this truth: If you want to advance, you must extend yourself. Advancing requires an active way of living on a day-to-day basis. Faith is about more than what you think and speak—it must extend to what you do. Faith without works is dead (James 2:26).

Many people think faith is hoping everything we need, want, and desire will fall out of the sky. Faith isn't wishing. It isn't even hoping. Faith is believing that what you want is lining up in the spiritual realm and coming toward you—and that spiritual force is happening as you actively and move toward your goal. When Paul says, "I press toward the mark," he is painting a very clear picture for us. He's letting us know there is always a mark—and a mark is specific. It's not vague.

As believers, we should be pressing toward a mark in our own lives—whatever that may be, whatever God has put on our heart, this mark needs to be clear to us. It can be small. It can be huge. But whatever the goal is, it needs to be specific and on point.

What do you want? Where do you want to go? What does success mean to you and why do you want it? What are you producing? Who are you becoming in the process? Are you living in joy, love, and peace as you press forward—and most importantly, is God first above it all? The answers to your questions should be specific and not vague. After all, if you don't know where you are going, how will you know when you get there?

"I press toward the mark for the prize of the high calling of God in Christ Jesus" shows us that Paul knew his mark was attached to a prize, and in his case, that prize was his calling. Paul greatly valued his ministry. And aren't you glad he did? Aren't you glad that he hit his mark? Today we know that two-thirds of the New Testament was written by Paul the apostle. The passion he had for his calling was necessary not only for his own life and destiny—but for all of us who are believers and rely upon his divinely-inspired, God-breathed words.

Paul also told us where his mark and prize were located—IN Christ Jesus. Your mark and your prize are also in Christ Jesus because the word "Christ" means Anointed One and His anointing. This means you will need to tap into the anointing in order to advance in what you want. The anointing is a game-changer. It's that divine spiritual energy and it is accessible through the power of the Holy Spirit dwelling in you.

CHAPTER 3

When You Advance Inwardly, It Shows Outwardly

Not long ago, a 14-year-old boy came up to me at a church I was visiting. I love kids and teenagers because they say exactly what is on their mind—they don't hold back. I'm amazed that at my age, I still so often meet young people who tell me they listen to my messages and enjoy the way that I preach. Now, I could tell as this boy walked up to me that he liked me because he just couldn't stop smiling at me.

The first words out of his mouth were, "Brother Jesse, you're cool." I was surprised and said, "Well, thank you…" and I couldn't say anymore because he cut me off with a question. "Why do you wear that tie like the old people?"

I looked at him and grabbed the turkey gizzard skin that hangs under my chin. I rumpled it up into a ball and tucked it into my shirt behind the tie he didn't like. "To keep THIS from falling down on my chest, boy!" I said. He started laughing so hard, so I gave him a word of wisdom about the future: "Don't laugh, boy," I told him, "It's going to happen to you, too, one day!"

Faith Produces an Inner Energy of Passion— It Keeps You Excited About What You're Doing Now, and Next!

I'm consistently told that I'm "not old"—but I know what I see when I look in the mirror. At one time, I had a six-pack, if you can believe it. And you will have to use your faith to believe it. Now? I have a keg. I can shake my head like those old cartoons and when I stop moving, the skin on my face is still moving. I do it for fun sometimes in the mirror. It makes me laugh. Why? Because I don't let aging get me down. It happens to the best of us because, well, it happens to all of us.

Like a doctor once told me when I asked him if there was any problem with my heart skipping a beat and starting strong again, "Well, Jesse, if it kicks back up again, it's better than the alternative." In other words, be happy you are alive! If it's still ticking, then you've got more to do.

I was born in 1949, and I've been preaching since 1978—and this earthly shell of a body isn't getting any younger. If my hair gets any whiter, it'll go clear. I don't have wrinkles; I have cracks. And, yeah, I have this turkey neck too...so I'm not young, but like I said, I'm consistently told I'm "not old." Why? I'm going to tell you why! It's because the life of God is pulsating in my spirit! I'm advancing! Not in years, though those are passing by—but in my mind and in my spirit, and in my calling, too.

Advancing in life means you aren't willing to let life pass you by. You are connected to your vision with passion, and always stoking the fires of your own God-given purpose in life. Whether it's what others would consider large or small, it doesn't matter—it's what

God put on your heart to do that matters for you. Because when you are doing that, you are going in the right direction.

We were not created to just barely make it and survive; we were created to enjoy life, to overcome the obstacles, and to live the adventure of faith. Faith in God changes everything.

My faith in God and my excitement about what I'm going to do with Him in this life is the spark of life that keeps me not just moving forward, but advancing. I believe that my own faith is exactly what keeps me "not old," even though I'm aging. Faith in God produces a mindset and an energy in me that makes me passionate about what I'm doing now, and what's coming next. Advancing inwardly shows outwardly.

The Word Is a Living Thing
It's God, It's Life, and It's the Light Inside of You

I love the Word of God. It's a living thing—divinely inspired words that bring an abundance of "life" to the hearer. As Hebrews 4:12 says, *"For the Word of God is quick, and powerful, and sharper than any twoedged sword, piercing even to the dividing asunder of soul and spirit, and of the joints and marrow, and is a discerner of the thoughts and intents of the heart."*

God is One with His Word—this is what gives the Word its power. It is not merely the words of men. It is inspired text. God-breathed text. The more you realize that God and His Word cannot be separated, the more you will value the Word for what it really is. Words of life from a Living God. These are words that bring light to the human spirit, mind, and body. And in men and women, the Word brings a light to the soul that others can see.

John 1:1-4 says it best: *"In the beginning was the Word, and the Word was with God, and the Word was God. The same was in the beginning with God. All things were made by Him; and without Him was not any thing made that was made. In Him was life; and the life was the light of men."*

The light of men is the life of God—and that life is One with the Word, which is why the Word can produce all sorts of wonderful things in your life. It's powerful because God Himself pulsates through His own Word. And yet, He has chosen faith as the vehicle we must use to activate the light and life of His Word. Faith pleases God. Without faith, it's actually impossible to please God. And when we have faith in Him, He rewards us for our diligence (Hebrews 11:6).

Not only does the light of God shining inside of you affect how others view you, but it is also what has the most effect on your own life. The more you have faith in the God who lives in you, the more you are going to let go of what is behind, and reach forward to what is ahead, and press toward the mark of whatever God has put in you to have or do.

Ask Yourself Some Heart-Questions And Be Diligent with Your Heart

Have you ever heard somebody say they have "issues"? We all have issues, and ALL the issues of everyone living this life spring from their own heart, according to Proverbs 4:23—which is why the same verse warns us to be diligent with our own heart.

The heart is the space God uses in people to impart true desires. The combination of faith in God's Word and following the true desires God has placed into your heart or spirit is always going to be your winning combo in life. You aren't here to goal for someone else's dreams and desires; you are here to believe for your own.

So, the question is: What has God put on your heart? What do you want? And if you ever worry about whether it's a true desire, just check with God and ask yourself what is your motivation for wanting it? Dream about it a bit! What are you going to do once you get it or once you are doing it?

The most important question, of course, is: Are you ready to stretch yourself toward whatever you are believing God for? Growth is required to advance with God because advancement doesn't just change your circumstances; it also changes you! It changes how you think, how you speak, and how you show up in your own life. It opens up even greater opportunities to bless, encourage, and help others in the world, too.

God has more for you. No matter how young or old you are, that is a fact! You wouldn't be breathing right now if that weren't true. If there is still life inside your body, then you've got more to do or more to say—something more to advance toward.

So, how do you advance? How do you get from "here" to "there" and do it with passion? Or even better than passion, with joy? Circumstances in life sometimes come like waves. You navigate those waves. It's God and you at the helm. But if you leave Him out or you just don't renew your mind, you won't feel in control of your own life at all. You'll feel like you're just hanging on, being beaten by the wind and waves, as the circumstances of your life whip you around. In other words, you'll live stressed out and make all your choices from a feeling of powerlessness.

God never meant you to feel powerless—you've got more power than you can shake a stick at because God is with you. Because He's with you, you are powerful, and it's that simple. That's the truth, whether you feel it or not. Feelings change all the time. And I've found that I can change how I feel simply by what I believe.

Focus on Your Foundation—Christ, the Hope of Glory

When I was praying one day about this advancing, the Lord told me, "Jesse, you must advance inwardly because if there is nothing in you, nothing can come out of you." We must recognize and not shy away from showing WHO is inside of us, *"...which is Christ in you, the hope of glory"* (Colossians 1:27).

If you have Christ inside of you, you also have hope inside of you. You have more hope available to you than you can even imagine—don't let the day's events steal that away. Stir up the gift of God inside yourself because that's advancing inwardly. We have been accepted by the Father. We have the Author of all life inside of us—and He is the starting point and the foundation of our life.

What's inside of you is more powerful than anything on this planet. Recognize the presence of God inside of you. Realize that His attributes are there, too—because when you tap into *"Christ in you, the hope of glory,"* you will find great confidence, and advancing His way will become pure joy.

People ask me all the time, "How do you stay so fired up? I know that you have trouble in life, but it seems like it just doesn't affect you." I say, "That's easy. I have the foundation of life living inside of me." You see, even in the natural world, when you have a good foundation, you can put all sorts of weight on that foundation and it will hold up and not crack.

The same is true in your spirit and soul because your foundation is *"Christ in you, the hope of glory."* Christ is living in you by the power of the Holy Spirit, so focus on that foundation. Realize that no matter what life throws, the God inside of you cannot break or crack—pull on the power of *"Christ in you, the hope of glory."*

Remember what Paul wrote in Philippians 3:14 and speak it out loud over yourself. Say, *"I press toward the mark for the prize of the high calling of God in Christ Jesus."* Life is a race—there are times you will sprint, times you will jog, and times that you may leisurely walk. But I believe this is a time to sprint! I don't care what anybody else has told you, you are a winner going somewhere to win because Christ in you, the hope of glory, has already won at the cross.

Who You Become Is Determined by What You Believe

Who you become is determined by what you believe about yourself. How you advance will be determined by what you do with that belief—it is not based on today's circumstances. Situations change all the time. Nothing is still. Nothing is stagnant…unless you are.

What you think about on a regular basis is what will create your desire to act or not act on what God has put in your heart. So, if you want to advance, you'll have to do some personal inventory. Ask yourself some questions.

What are you focused on? Is it what you want or what you don't want? What are you thinking about on a repetitive basis? Are you energized by those thoughts? Are they in line with what God said you could do and have? If the thoughts manifested right now, would you want what you are thinking about?

Are your thoughts advancing you or holding you back? Are they stirring up the gift of God that is in you to advance or distracting you from pressing toward the mark? In the next chapter, I'm going to tell you what I do inwardly so that I can advance outwardly in the visions and goals God gives me.

CHAPTER 4

I Create My World and I Live in It

No matter what area you want to advance in life, you need to go there "inside" first. To succeed, I decided long ago that I would create my world—and live in it. Period. Now, when I say I create my own world and live in it, I mean I create my own inner world using the Word of God and exercise the confidence that faith in His Word gives me.

The anointing of God rests on His Word. Never discount the anointing of God on His Word. The Word of God is anointed—and that anointing is transferable to your spirit, your mind, and your body.

There is a very energetic quality to faith that has the power to move natural circumstances and manifest things—you simply cannot do without it. The anointing of God that rests on His Word will flow through you. All you have to do is have faith in God and use the anointed Word to transform your own mind. It's part of what I call, "creating my own world and living in it."

To create your own world and live in it as a believer is to fully value and use the Word of God. The teachings, principles, and admonitions in the Word of God are invaluable to me. The Word is part of my everyday life.

I consider every scripture I read, every passage I meditate on, and every principle I follow to be "sowing to the spirit" like Galatians 6:8 and I reap new thoughts, new words, and new possibilities. The Word that I sow into myself inspires the words I say and the choices I make.

My faith in the Word literally manifests miracles in my life, but it also draws new choices into my life. Choices to advance. I'm not a baby, and God doesn't treat me like one. I'm full-grown, and while He will simply place some things into my life, other things He requires me to use my faith to draw it in.

You see, it's up to me every day to stir up the gift of God within me and to stoke the fires of my spirit with the Word—to not only read the Word but become one with the Word so that I can take divinely-inspired action when opportunities come. That's the inner work I do so that the outer work of pressing toward the mark in everyday actions stays on target with what I believe.

I am not interested in advancing outside of God's ways—that is not true advancement to me. I am interested in reaching my destination and fulfilling my destiny with Him at the center of my life. And I stay true to the goals He's put in front of me by keeping my eyes pointed in the right direction.

The Eye of the Soul Must Be Fixed on Jesus

I like the way Hebrews 12:2 puts it—it says, *"Looking unto Jesus the Author and Finisher of our faith…"* Getting to the finish line of any project God puts on my heart is done by "looking," and that look is a believing look unto Jesus. It brings transformation to my mind, and makes all things possible to me.

The eye of the soul must be fixed upon Jesus. Pressing toward the mark in our life is going to be much easier if Jesus is our first and primary focus. He gave us the "pattern" for how to love others, how to speak, and how to dwell with others in this life—and He also gave us the pattern for how to handle struggles and deal with the attacks of people and the devil.

Look at what you are wearing right now. Someone somewhere was involved in the creation of those clothes. For each piece, there was someone who had to cut the material to make it, and they used a "pattern" to do it. The piece of clothing will match whatever pattern it was cut from.

The more we are *"looking unto Jesus"* the more we will start to believe His way, think His way, love His way, and do things His way. Our faith will match His pattern. This is how He fulfills His role as *"the Author and Finisher of our faith."* He can't be the Author or the Finisher unless we are consistently looking unto Him.

I Don't Pray Long, But I Don't Go Long Without Praying

A lot of people ask me how long I pray every day and are surprised when I say, "I don't pray long..." You see, I know some people like to pray long lengths of time, but I'm not one of them. Of course, I always add, "...but I don't go long without praying." I have a habit of talking to God off and on throughout my day.

I take a lot more time to put the Word into my mind and heart because that is learning. I'm understanding and gaining wisdom through the Word. I'm reprogramming my mind to think rightly. But prayer is communication, and since I'm born again, I love that I get to live in a regular communication with the Lord.

I don't need to save up my "prayers" for when I talk to the Lord next—because I'll likely talk to Him in a few seconds. He's inside of me. I pray all the time, not for long, but for as long as I want to, and

I don't care who's around because I silently talk to Him all the time. He is always with me—He never leaves me or forsakes me (Hebrews 13:5). So, I talk to Him on my treadmill, in my car, in my office, or wherever I want to.

He stirs me up and keeps me focused. He lifts me up and encourages me. If I need wisdom, I ask for it like James 1:5 says and He is faithful to give it to me liberally and ungrudgingly, without reproach or faultfinding. But I'd never get the wisdom I need if I didn't read His Word or talk to Him. Learning and communicating with Him is critical to advancing.

I share my thoughts with God. I reason with Him to get clarity. If I'm irritated, I let it out on God—He knows anyway! He's not surprised! But in letting out whatever I have on my mind, I am able to then receive what He says to me. I tap into what 1 Corinthians 2:16 calls "the mind of Christ," which means the anointed mind that "knows all things." Remember, "Christ" means Anointed and His anointing. To have His "mind" is to have an anointed mind.

Realize that you have an inward guide at all times because of Jesus. Inside of you, right now, you've got a Comforter, a Counselor, a Savior, and a Friend. Sowing the Word into your mind reprograms you to think at a higher level—a divine level. But *"looking unto Jesus"* as the Author and Finisher of your faith helps you tap into the anointing, and in that anointing is the answer for whatever comes up in life. There is no obstacle too hard for "the mind of Christ" to handle.

So, making a habit of consistently *"looking unto Jesus"* will transform your thinking and will bring those dreams, visions, and goals that are inside of you into real and lasting focus. Even if you get distracted, or need to blow off steam, or need clarity or wisdom, *"looking unto Jesus"* will help you.

My "World" Is Peaceful Even When It's Busy

His burden is easy and His yoke is light, as Matthew 11:30 says. So, turning to Jesus in your everyday life may need to become a new habit, but it's an easy habit to get into. It makes advancing lighter work because He does not bring a spirit of heaviness and drudgery— He lightens the heart and mind. He makes impossible things doable, without mental strain and pain.

"Looking unto Jesus" is a more peaceful way to advance—because with Jesus, nothing you do comes out of a place of fear. If it's His Spirit guiding you, it's a spirit of power, love, and peace. Worry, anxiety, and mental stress is the junk that *"looking unto Jesus"* relieves you from. So just get into the habit.

"Looking unto Jesus" is my daily practice. It energizes me not only for whatever I've scheduled myself to do today, but it's also how I gain joy and peace to persevere toward huge goals I know that I cannot do alone or in my own strength.

Just knowing that I can't do it on my own is a relief. That's when I have to put my faith in God—and the longer I've been living this way, the bigger and bigger the projects He gives me seem to get! It's exciting. Faith in God is what gives me the tenacity to persevere because tenacity is needed to manifest anything.

ADVANCE by Persevering in Well Doing— Find Your Spiritual and Mental Energy in Jesus

I love tenacity and perseverance. Anybody can quit and give up, but it's those who persevere that make things happen. You won't burn up or burn out with God's plan for your life, unless you start running it all on your own. Don't run on your own!

I like to say that it's easy to start running, but it's harder to keep running. To do well, we all need to be inspired regularly. To persevere, we all need to be energized. And guess Who does that better than anyone else? JESUS.

Guess Who believes in you more than anyone else? JESUS. Guess Who will breathe energy into your day and help you to persevere in well doing so that you keep running your race until you get to the end? JESUS! If you are worn out, you are doing the running on your own. It's time to start *"looking unto Jesus"* more than ever. Your power lies in your connection to Christ. He is your Source.

Talking to Him, studying the Word, and praying in the Holy Spirit will keep you running—even if the goal is long-range. You'll actually speed up the manifestation time if you decide that perseverance itself is worth the gain of whatever you're believing for.

It's a bottom line fact that you will learn something about yourself in the persevering time. You learn where you need to get stronger in your faith. You'll see the moments when you want to give up—and you'll learn how to turn right back to Jesus, right back to the Word, and right back to what you want. You'll find out if what you want is important enough for you to persevere. I pray it is!

Because when you persevere, you are learning how patience works—it matures in you by practice, and at the end of patience is the "wanting nothing" state (James 1:4). Not because you give up—but because you manifest whatever it is that you were wanting in the first place. Patience is part of persevering. It's part of the process of faith in God. And it's required.

The good thing is that patience is a fruit of the Spirit of God—so it's in you because the Spirit of God is in you, and that means you are capable. *"Looking unto Jesus"* helps you to rest in Him, knowing that the "lag-time" of manifestation isn't without purpose. Something is happening—both in you and in the spiritual realm to bring you what you want. The process is just as important as the end goal. Never forget that.

Talk to the Lord. Study the Word. Remind yourself of what He has told you. Have faith in God and faith in yourself, and the perseverance to keep pressing toward your mark will rise up to meet the challenges of your race. Once you know that patience and perseverance are just part of it, it makes it much easier to keep running your race in life with joy.

There is one thing people can never say about me and that's that I'm lazy—it's just not in my DNA. Part of the reason for that is because I consistently sow to the Spirit instead of the flesh. *"Looking unto Jesus"* is fuel for my soul. It helps my mind, my will, and my emotions—it's what gives me tenacity. *"Looking unto Jesus"* is what gives me the spiritual and mental energy to persevere as I keep on pressing toward the mark.

Faith Is the Match, the Anointing Is the Fire— What You Believe Changes Everything

Now, it must be said: You can read scripture or listen to messages all day long, you can even talk to the Lord. But if you don't believe and you don't move, you will not advance. You can't just absorb information, you must apply it. Faith must be active, and without works, it's dead.

If faith is a match, the anointing of God is the fire that erupts when you strike that match on the Word—it's "I believe, therefore I speak" and "I believe, therefore I act." If you want to advance, you have to strike that match. You have to allow the anointing that rises when you read or speak the Word to come up and out of your recreated spirit. It will light you up from the inside. And from your spirit and that light, the fire of the Holy Spirit will shine its purifying light on your mind and your path.

You'll step more confidently in the direction of your goals and dreams. You'll be able to recognize opportunities that manifest themselves—because opportunity follows faith in God. When that happens, take action.

You are anointed to make the right choices. The Holy Spirit will tap you in the heart if something is not right. Because you've been putting the Word into your spirit and talking with the Lord, what is not right will be obvious to you. Heed the Spirit within you. The ball is in your court, every day, regardless of circumstances. Free will is never out of play.

You are anointed to reach your own goals. You are anointed to fulfill your destiny and reach your destination. But it's always going to be faith that creates the spark—faith in God, faith in His Word, and faith in yourself, too.

When faith in God, His Word, and yourself becomes a priority, you will kindle the divine energy that changes things—but never forget, it changes you inwardly before it ever changes what's going on outwardly.

It is something others can feel. The energy of faith is an amazing thing. It charges the atmosphere around you with a higher level of energy that produce feelings of hope, joy, mercy, peace, or power. It brings favor into your life. It makes you confident. Because what you believe changes everything.

People you come in contact with might not know why, but they will recognize that something about you is different than average people just going through the motions of life. What's different? Faith and the anointing are in action within you. You are advancing inwardly and it's showing outwardly. You are creating your own world and living in it!

It Looks Like a Passion for Life, It's Really the Fullness of God Emanating from Your Spirit

Faith has a pure "pulling up" effect that shakes off the cobwebs of the natural mind! Faith eliminates confusion. Faith in God's Word causes you to replace old, tiring thoughts with new, God-driven thoughts about you, your family, and your future—these thoughts create your own inner world.

"For as he thinketh in his heart, so is he" is found in Proverbs 23:7. This is a great scriptural truth because it is exactly what you think and what you believe that will pave the way for how you speak and what you do. So, cultivating an inner world is vital to advancing God's way. In fact, you can't advance God's way without doing it.

What you think matters. What you believe matters. Moment by moment, thought by thought, and action by action, you are moving one direction or another. I want to challenge you to move in a forward and upward direction because this is God's best for you. I want to see you create the spark with your own faith so that the anointing of God that rests on His Word shines through you.

When you live by letting Him shine out of you, you are creating your own inner world that is in sync with God, and your life becomes much more fulfilling—right here and now—not just when you reach your goals or fulfill your dreams, but now. Faith in God and the anointing of God brings fullness into your heart. It affects your emotions in a wonderful way, too.

Living this way looks like confidence or a passion for life to some people, but it's really being in alignment with the Lord and living with His anointing on your life—it's His fullness emanating from your own spirit. Others are drawn towards it because the energy it creates is real. It renews your youth according to Psalm 103:5 so that you soar like the eagles—in other words, above Christian turbulence!

To live this way makes you like a magnet. Not only will you start accomplishing and receiving more of what you are believing for by manifesting your own needs and desires, but you'll also start being a magnet for people who need what you have—and that is God.

You'll draw people onto your path who need what you have, or at least want to be closer to it. You'll draw unbelievers. You'll draw believers who have gotten weary, too. So, not only will creating your own world and living in it help you to build faith, persevere in patience, act on golden opportunities and manifest what you want in life, but it will also open a door to share your faith.

Real faith in God is a game-changer, and holding onto it is key. Now, let's talk about what happens when your natural mind pops up and tries to steal your future with fear.

What Do You Believe About Your Future? It's What You Say to Yourself that Matters Most

The most important part of your life is what you believe about your future—so what do you believe about your future? When you think about it, what comes up first? For many people, fear comes up first. They imagine the worst, so of course, they fall into all sorts of distractions—they work against themselves in the mind before they have a chance to believe God for His best.

If sad, sick, disgusted, and busted is what you think, guess what you are going to produce in life? You got it! You'll get what you believe for. You'll get what you intend to receive. Your own faith will work against God's best interest for you.

I like to say that if you aren't talking about your good vision, your not-so-good vision will be talking about you—it'll talk for you in the form of where you are going in you own life. You see, you can say all sorts of good things around people, but it's what you say to yourself that matters the most. What you say to yourself, about yourself, and about your future is what is going to show up in your life, no matter how good you sound to others.

Advancement, regardless of the area, requires that you think higher, change, and adapt. It's not easy because it requires something of you, but the prize is great! It's worth the effort of thinking differently and stirring yourself up to take whatever productive action is necessary to advance in your vision.

So, what do you believe about yourself and your future? What do you believe about yourself as you get older? If you say, "Well, you know, Mama had diabetes, Daddy had diabetes, and you know, cancer and heart attacks run in my family, so…" well then, now you know what you are believing for your own future. Now, if you don't want that stuff, stop talking about it like you do. That's what you will manifest in some way or another.

You can choose what you will believe about your future. From that inward choice, you will make outward choices. You'll decide to think better thoughts, God's thoughts about your future—which are plans to give you hope, not dread! (Jeremiah 29:11) Those thoughts will cause you to want to say words that match what you want—which is health.

You might find yourself confessing Word-based things like, "Your Word is in my heart, God, and it's life to my spirit and health to my body! I speak pleasant words because they are like honey—sweet to my soul and health to my bones! God, you are always with me! You deliver me, honor me, and satisfy me with long life. You continually show me the goodness of Your salvation. My body is wonderfully made and I walk in divine health today!"

You see, it's hard to take actions against yourself when you are thinking good thoughts and saying good words. Every day, in that respect, your thoughts are paving the way for your words, and your words are paving the way for your actions. Your future is in your mind and your mouth first. And every action you take is a step either in the direction you want or the direction you don't want.

Death and life are in the power of the tongue, and the scripture says that they who love it eat the fruit of it (Proverbs 18:21). In other words, what you say matters. And you can tell what you love by what you say. Now, you may not like the eventual outcome—who really wants death? But that doesn't matter. It's about what *you* keep on saying over and over and over; because that is an indicator of what you believe about your own future. You are speaking the future into existence—why not speak life? Speak good things over yourself. Your future literally depends on it. Your joy and peace for today, right now, depends on it, too.

CHAPTER 5

"Catch" Your Thoughts: Don't Deny Reality, Choose Truth

In 40 years of full-time ministry, I have never had a financial deficit. Isn't that a miracle of God? At present, 2.9 billion people today have access to the messages I broadcast in 14 different languages on television around the world. That's not counting social media. This is a huge financial undertaking—and when other ministers or business people ask, "How do you do it? Even recessions don't seem to affect you!" I give them the answer. I don't "undertake" the financial burden—I'm not under it, and I don't take it!

You see, I've learned the truth. I'm in the world, but I'm not of it. I didn't memorize faith—I learned it. When you learn things, you remember things. When you memorize things, you forget them as soon as the test is over.

My faith in the anointed Word of God is the key to my success—and "success," for me, isn't just spiritual, it isn't just physical, and it isn't just financial. It's all three and much more. We are spirit beings. We have bodies. We live in an economic world. To aim for only one kind of advancement isn't God's best to me.

God's best is whole. It's full. It encompasses the best parts of our life. It's only limited by what we choose to focus upon and what we'll settle for. I don't want to settle. I may direct my focus more strongly in one area than another for a time because I'm working on something, but I do not want to leave out anything God has for me or the work I'm called to do.

I don't delude myself or deny reality. That's not what creating your own world and living in it means. This is not about denying the circumstances. It's about denying their right to remain if they aren't lining up with the truth of God's Word or what you are believing Him for.

In other words, I choose truth regardless of reality—and I speak the end result. That's how I use my faith, and I see it change circumstances that were once reality. It creates new circumstances. It manifests results. Living by faith in this way is totally contrary to how most people think and live. Most people are always striving and pushing to attain something outwardly, while not paying much attention to what's going on inwardly. But I've learned that the spirit and soul trumps the physical—and I've got to put them first if I want to advance.

Manifestations of my faith sometimes come quickly. Sometimes they come in time. I'm always ahead of what I see today—because I want to build a better tomorrow, and that starts now. Not in fear or worry, but in faith. You see, you cannot advance if you don't look where you are going. You especially can't advance if you look only at where you've been. The past never sees the future.

"Catch" Your Thoughts Before They Seed— Bring Every Thought into Captivity to the Obedience of Christ

One of the greatest things I ever did for myself and for the ministry God has placed in my care was deciding to trust God—not vaguely in words but fully in thoughts, words, and actions. I've convinced myself that God can't lie! And so, every time a thought rises up in me that says otherwise, I do what the Word says and bring it into captivity (2 Corinthians 10:5). To bring a thought into "captivity" means you've got to catch it—you can't just let it bat around your head and seed itself into your heart.

That means you must take the controls back and turn them over to the anointing of Christ. When you catch yourself thinking something that is totally not in line with God's Word or the dream, goal, or life you want—bring that thought into captivity. Catch it. Put your mind back into obedience to Christ's anointing and on what He's placed on your heart to have or to do in life.

Now, you can't just push thoughts out and sit around thinking nothing. Your brain doesn't work that way. So, work with what you've been given and start replacing doubtful thoughts with what the Word says and what you want. When I do this, I'm NOT trying to convince myself of anything. I'm not denying or arguing with reality. I'm reminding myself of what is TRUE.

Reality is one thing. Truth is another. I have a mindset for success because I know that reality will bend to the truth—because with God, all things are possible to them who believe (Mark 9:23). I'm a believer, so all things are possible. Miracles happen every day. They aren't dropped down from Heaven. They are created right here on earth from our recreated spirits when the reality we see bends and is changed by the truth of God.

So, I create my world by aligning my mind and my spirit with what God says and not with what my own mind wants to drift toward or what other people say about my advancement. People say all sorts of trash! People don't believe most of the time. Even great Christians will often think they are helping me out by stirring up doubt and fear with words that don't line up with what God said in His Word.

I decided a long time ago that if God called me to the ministry, He would help me fulfill the vision He gave me. He would provide the people I needed to help me do the work. He would pay for whatever is needed to fulfill His plan and His work—including television costs. And He has. And He keeps doing it.

If you are a believer, and you want to advance in anything God has put on your heart, stop arguing with reality and just start choosing the truth. Make it a habit to catch thoughts that don't align, and replace them with thoughts that do—speak it out.

Don't argue with yourself. Don't overthink it. Just shift your thoughts. Choose what God says in the Word. Choose what He put on your heart. Make it an everyday discipline to actively choose what is true over whatever is the current reality—and one day, you will see the manifestation of what you believe. Faith and the anointing of God working in the mind and mouth of a believer changes reality.

Most People I Meet Want More Money— You Can't Experience Abundance if All You Think About is Lack

Now, most people I meet need or want more money—because again, we live in an economic world. In fact, the only two places where it seems like money is not used are in Heaven and on Star Trek. People want to know how to create more finances. I share spiritual principles about finances because that is what has worked and continues to work for me—I believe that all external problems are connected to internal problems.

When I was growing up in poverty as a kid, I really thought money would make me happy. So, I grew up. I wasn't saved, but

I made a lot of money as a musician in the early 1970s. To me, I had more money than I ever dreamed of as a kid. I wasn't happy at all. You see, just because you get what you want doesn't mean you'll satisfy the core reason of why you wanted it in the first place—that's why so many people end up feeling dissatisfied, even when they get what they want.

As believers, we aren't like people who have no God (Ephesians 2:12-13). We know what God can do! So, why do so many believers still end up dissatisfied when they make financial goals their priority and get them? Because, even as a Christian, many fall into the trap of only chasing a "thing"—and not chasing the One who anointed them for abundance in the first place. God must be first if you are a believer. Everything else, and I do mean everything else, must come second—because if you want to advance God's way, you must put God first (Matthew 6:33). That's what He requires.

This means truth must come first. Money won't set you free. A relationship won't set you free. Health won't set you free. You can have all of those things and still be bound up, living in mental lack, and without peace of mind or joy in your heart.

Only the truth will set you free—and not just the truth on its own sitting in the Bible on a shelf, but the truth you dig into and KNOW. *"And ye shall know the truth, and the truth shall make you free"* (John 8:32). It's the truth you've internalized, the truth you've accepted, and the truth that moves you to action that will set you FREE. There is no freedom in half-heartedly believed truth.

This is why I'm not interested in just "memorizing" the truth and parroting things back to myself without faith—plenty of people do that and that's why it doesn't work. Faith isn't a formula. It's a force and an energy that all of us are capable of using, and it's meant to be hooked up to the God who is the Source of everything.

I'm interested in learning God's truth, not just memorizing it. I am interested in receiving God's truth deep into my heart, and then believing God's truth by renewing my mind daily—and then simply trusting that He meant what He said. What He said, He will do! If I do my part and get my inner world in order, my outer world will shape up and conform to the truth that I know. I will see manifestation.

I study the Word. I speak it with my mouth. I choose to live as if all my prayers have already been answered because that's faith in God to do what He said. Remember that Jesus said, *"Therefore I say unto you, What things soever ye desire, when ye pray, believe that ye receive them, and ye shall have them"* (Mark 11:24).

So, you must "believe that ye receive them" before you move into "shall have them." I pray you are getting this! I pray that you are understanding that faith is "living in reverse"—it's believing before seeing, and it's a better way to live because it harnesses the power that Jesus told us we could use in order to create changes in our own lives.

Age Has Nothing to Do with "Newness of Life"— You Can Learn, Grow, and Produce at Any Age

Age means nothing when it comes to faith and imagination—I don't care if you are "old" and just learning to use faith. Better now than never! God can use you. And if you are young, you are learning a God-concept that will make your life so much more enjoyable.

People are too quick to discount themselves according to their age on a calendar. We are going to live forever. So, if you start living with hope and joy in the faith God gave you early in your earthly life or later in your earthly life, just be glad you started. It's one less thing you'll have to learn in Heaven!

I've had people tell me, "Yeah, but Brother Jesse, I'm already 80 years old." They think their life is done. It's not! Your time on earth is done when your time on earth is done! You aren't "done" ahead of time. There is an appointed time for all to die, and God alone knows that time. So if you are here, there is a reason and God can use you, regardless of age, to do something great—and to enjoy your life in the process. Don't let the number on your birth certificate fool you into thinking any other way. Moses started in the ministry when he was 80 years old. Abraham didn't do his best till he was 100 years old!

You need to radiate new life every day—I don't care how old or young you are. Age has nothing to do with it. God created you, and He didn't do it so that you would live down in the dumps and bored. You are a new creature in Christ, and that means *"newness of life"* is available to you in God, in His Word, and in following the dictates of the dreams, visions, and goals He has placed in your heart (2 Corinthians 5:17; Romans 6:4).

Many people have been following my ministry for years. I have many friends and acquaintances who have known me for over 40 and 50 years even—not one of them can tell you that they've seen me wallowing in misery, no matter what has been going on in my life. And a lot has gone on!

The devil has no new tricks and attacks come to everyone, but I've read the end of the Book—and we win. So, whatever life throws might be a challenge, but I refuse to let it kick me into the dirt. I ask my friends, "Have you ever seen me discouraged? Disappointed? Despondent? Sick? Broke?" They say no every time. You see, I decided I wanted the whole enchilada—I didn't want to go to Heaven but live a miserable life here on earth.

If there is peace of mind in God, I want it. If there is hope and power in God, I want it. If there is freshness of life in God, I want it. So, I engage in the discipline of cultivating not just a relationship but also a fellowship with my Lord. It's important to me! We can learn, grow, and produce the results we want at any age. Don't ever let anyone tell you that you are too young or too old to produce. Faith works for everybody, regardless of age.

ADVANCE IN LIFE

CHAPTER 6

If You Want to Advance, Don't Identify with What Holds You Back

It seems like the Christian world starts from the wrong perspective when it comes to growth. They fixate on problems and spend all their time moaning about it, instead of doing what Jesus did when it came to creating change.

Jesus had faith in God. Jesus prayed. Jesus got alone with God to recoup and feed His spirit more intensely. Jesus didn't just talk about the problem—He spoke TO the problem. Jesus spoke the end result and commanded problems to come into proper alignment with God's truth and line up with what He wanted to happen.

Fixating on the problem does nothing but keep you bound up in the mental and emotional components of that problem. Focusing on the solution is Christ's way. And Christ's way will move your thoughts, words, and actions toward the Word of God, toward the principles of that Word, and toward the solution to the problem. What you fixate on becomes your reality, and it happens first in your mind.

The truth is Jesus went to the cross! Jesus gave us the victory! We are victors and not victims. We are whole and not broken—because of what Jesus did at the cross, so stop "working on yourself" from an "I'm broken" mentality. Change your perspective. Don't try and make any changes from the negative. Start with the truth and let the truth change what's negative. It's not your job to rework the wheel. God can help you if you let Him, but nothing changes outwardly without that inward change of mentality first.

Let's face it, the more people focus on what they don't like about themselves, the more sick, more sad, and more disgusted they get with themselves. Rehashing misery just stirs up more misery. I look at it this way: If I could change myself all on my own, I wouldn't need faith in God because I'd have already done the impossible myself! I can't. God is necessary. Nothing is impossible WITH God, so the opposite must be true, too (Luke 1:37).

God must be at the core of any change you or I want to see in life—personal change within the believer's life must include God. You'd be amazed at how many Christians ignore this fact and just keep beating themselves up for not being this way or that way.

So, what do I do when I want to see changes in myself? I choose to focus on truth. I don't focus on where I am; I focus on where I'm going and what I want. I push myself to think toward the end result—because again, that's faith in God. And again, faith is acting like your prayers have already been answered—and that includes the desire to change something within myself. It's about identification.

Stop Wrongly Labeling Yourself—Identify with Christ Accept and Honor the Work of the Cross

One of the biggest mistakes I see believers make is to keep identifying with the problems in their life or their past. They live under a label that isn't true and don't even realize that their whole mindset is polluted by untrue identification.

As Christians, we should identify with Christ. We should not only accept the work of the cross, but also honor the work of the cross. We do this every time we agree with and align ourselves with what the Word says about us—not what anybody else has said about us, not what the world may have said about us, or even what we have said about ourselves!

For instance, a lot of people walk around calling themselves sinners. I don't do this. Why? I'm not a sinner because Jesus paid the price on the cross for my sin, and that makes me the Redeemed of the Lord. I am the Redeemed of the Lord, and that's the truth because that's what Jesus has done for me. That's the grace of God in effect.

I refuse to call myself a sinner because while I may have sinned, the blood of Jesus has washed my sin away. My identity is no longer in the sin—it's in the Savior! My identity is not in any problem—it's in the solution! And that solution is found in the blood of Jesus that paved the way for my success spiritually, physically, and in every other way. That solution is also found in the teachings of Jesus and the principles of the holy Word of God. I like to identify with truth.

Jesus did the work, and now it's our job to believe and advance in life. We do that by the very act of believing and then taking actions based on those beliefs. So, no, I'm not broken and neither are you! I'm not even cracked, and neither are you! Why? Because of Jesus. Because of the cross.

If you have given your heart to the Lord, you are far from broken. You need to change your perspective to see yourself through the blood of Jesus and what He has done for you. Period. Drop those bad labels! Because of what Jesus did, you and I can live as the victors, the champions in our own lives. We can do what God says we can do. We can have what God says we can have. We should not identify ourselves with what Jesus redeemed us from on the cross at Calvary.

I like to insert myself into the scriptures and make the Word personal like this. Let's say I'm using Isaiah 53:5-6 as my verse. I'll say something like, "Jesus, You were wounded for my transgressions. You were bruised for my iniquity. The chastisement for my peace was put on You. And by the stripes laid on Your back, I am healed. Like everybody else in life, I've gone astray. Like everyone, I've done things my own way. Thank You, Jesus, that You took all sin, missteps, sickness, fear, and anxiety onto Your body on the cross. I don't have to walk in any of that—I'm free and clear because You paid the price. Today, I'm walking in my blood-bought victory. I'm walking in the truth! Nothing is in my way and nothing is holding me back. I am redeemed! Clear and pure because of what You did! Thank You, Jesus!"

I'll do this same thing with any other subject. When I need favor, I'll insert myself again. I might use Psalm 5:12 or Proverbs 8:35 and say something like, "You are blessing me, God! You bless me because I'm righteous before You, and Your favor surrounds me like a shield—everywhere I go, I have favor because I am blessed! I have found Your wisdom, God, and it's through Your wisdom that I am enjoying life and favor!" I also like Luke 2:52: "Like Jesus, You are helping me to have great wisdom and favor, with both God and man—everywhere I go, I have favor!"

If I am believing for more finances or wealth, I'll use verses like Proverbs 13:22: "The wealth of the sinner is laid up for Jesse! Thank You, God, for causing me to be so wealthy that I leave an inheritance for my children's children!" I might use, James 1:4, "Thank You, God, that Your patience is working in me—it's perfecting me. I'm going to a place where I am mature, entire, and wanting nothing because I have everything!"

I may also use Luke 16:13, and 3 John 2: "I don't serve money, I serve God—and because I serve God, money isn't a problem for me. Thank You, God, for making it Your favorite wish that I prosper and be in health, even as my soul—my mind, will, and emotions—prospers!" I also love Isaiah 45:2-3: "Thank You for going before me, God, and making the crooked places straight! Break what keeps me in. Show me. You are giving me treasures, even in the darkness, and the hidden riches of secret places!"

What am I doing by using scriptures and putting myself in them? I'm not only speaking the life-giving energy of the Word of God, but I am personally identifying with what it says I can do, have, and be. The options for this are endless. No matter what the subject, no matter what you need, desire, or want to make happen or stop happening, there is a verse you can use. Identify with it! Use it.

I speak the Word over myself in the morning. I put a verse or a passage in my head before bed. When things come up against me, I then have the Word to pull on because it's in me. I've identified with it to such a degree that it just rises up in me to meet challenges that come up.

So, I encourage you to think about what you are identifying with. Be careful with what you allow to define you as a believer. Don't fall into the trap of thinking about the current circumstances so much that you negate the truth of God. You have so much at your disposal with the Word, and your identity is in Christ and in the teachings of the Word that bring life.

Never forget that what you give the most attention to are the "thought-seeds" you are sowing into your own heart and mind—and your outward future is in your inward seed. You will manifest. The root of that seed will spring up and produce, good or bad. Make no mistake.

"Be not deceived; God is not mocked: for whatsoever a man soweth, that shall he also reap" (Galatians 6:7). This applies financially, of

course, and I've written and spoken from the financial aspect many times before, but this verse also applies to every single thing we do—including repetitive thoughts and words.

That means the harvest of your thought-seeds will be a multiplication of whatever you are consistently identifying with—what is on your mind, what is coming out of your mouth, and what you are doing on a consistent basis.

What's the bottom line? If you want to advance, don't identify with what will hold you back! If you want to advance, don't label yourself as something you do not want to be! Use the Word and identify with what brings encouragement, joy, peace, faith, and more—make it a habit and then live like what you want has already happened. In other words, live like you believe it!

An Advance Mindset Focuses on the End Result— Act Like Your Prayers Have Already Been Answered

What does "acting like your prayers have already been answered" mean? It means you focus on the truth that you will one day manifest in reality. It means that, right now, you decide to use your godly imagination and allow yourself to feel it in your heart as if it has already happened.

Choose end-result thoughts. Rehearse them in your mind. Allow yourself to dream and imagine. Your body will get with the program and produce emotions to coincide with your own thoughts—and who doesn't want to feel good? That's a benefit of faith. You can feel good now, before you even manifest it.

Have you ever had a bad dream and woke up sweating and with your heart beating hard? Your brain will produce emotions in accordance with your thoughts. This means if you drag yourself down inwardly, you'll feel it outwardly. And if you lift yourself up inwardly, you'll feel it outwardly, too. Why not enjoy feeling good?

When you manifest what you want, it'll be exciting, but you'll find that it's not much more exciting than the emotions you felt the whole time you were believing God for it in the first place! Why? Again, because when you believe by faith, before anything manifests, you feel as if the prayer has already been answered.

Do you notice that the Word doesn't record Jesus acting crazily excited by His own miracles and manifestations? And have you noticed how He'd tell people they should have more faith when they marveled so much at what His faith in God produced? Think about that. It's because it was "done" in His heart and mind before it happened in reality.

Allow yourself to feel the emotions of actually having it—imagine it, let it roll over and over. That's your God-given imagination working for you and with you, instead of against you. Remember, an advance mindset is a faith mindset. Faith is calling those things that be not as though they were, until they are (Romans 4:17).

So, think like it's done in your mind. Talk like it's done to yourself. Go further even and say "Thank You" to God. Exercise appreciation before it manifests by thanking the Lord for the end result. This is a key to unlocking your manifestation.

"Accurate" Isn't the Same As "Truth"

I realize this might seem crazy or feel tough to do—especially if you have a lifetime of natural programming. Your brain might pop up and tell you, "But that's just not true! I am sick!" or "I am broke!" or whatever. Your mind does this because it's trained to notice what is accurate. It's not trained to notice what is true. You see, your emotions are accurate. You feel the way you feel. But just because you can accurately describe your feelings doesn't make them true—they are just accurate!

For most people, until they start renewing their mind to the Word and learn what is true, they will live by the facts of life or the accuracy of their own emotions. This means they will not immediately focus on the truth. They will just naturally focus on what they don't have, haven't done, or every other opposite and negative aspect of their life. The natural brain picks out flaws and calls it as it sees it. Faith is a higher way of thinking.

To advance, you need to realize that thoughts come and go, but the believer's life is marked by what is true. Let me explain. Thoughts and emotions that come from the "natural mind" may be accurate to what they are—but that doesn't make them true. What God says is true.

For instance, the natural mind may think, "I'm at the bottom, I'll never be at the top. I feel like a loser"—and hey, that might be accurate to how you feel or think naturally! But it's NOT the truth. The truth is the Word: "I am the head and not the tail, above and not beneath…I am more than a conquer and I can do all things through Christ" (Deuteronomy 28:13; Romans 8:37; Philippians 4:13).

Your natural mind may say, *I'll never have what I need.* But the truth of God says, *"But my God shall supply all your need according to His riches in glory by Christ Jesus"* (Philippians 4:19). Your natural mind might say, "I'm sick and miserable and my body doesn't work right!" but the truth is "My body is a temple. It's wonderfully made and it works! By the stripes laid on Jesus' back, healing flows through me and makes everything whole and complete!" (1 Corinthians 6:19; Psalm 139:14; Isaiah 53:5)

Do you see what I'm talking about? "Sick" might be a fact and be completely accurate—but "healed" is the truth! "Broke" might be a very accurate assessment of your finances—but "blessed" is the truth! So, when your mind pops off at you as you start confessing the truth, don't get flustered and resist it—just hit the pause button in your head and realize that's just your natural brain trying to figure things out. It's not accustomed to faith yet!

Cut yourself some slack and remind yourself that you are working on something. Don't fight your own mind. Just shift your focus back to the truth. Tell yourself, "Regardless of the problem, the truth is my solution." Then go back to speaking the Word or what you want. Move that thought. If you don't move those thoughts to the truth, you'll just keep manifesting the same old junk that you don't want.

Thoughts that are not in line with the truth are worthless because they keep you stuck. Whatever is true, good, healthy, and right in God's sight is invaluable because they shift your perspective to set you free (Philippians 4:8). Developing an advance mindset in this way sets you free from "stuck" because it takes the labels and limits off. Truth and faith set into motion a divine energy that goes to work on your behalf.

Take the Limits Off of Your Own Advancement

For your entire life, people may have been telling you what you "can't do" or "can't have." Most successful people have heard that at one time or another, and many people in the world have heard it all their lives.

I grew up poor and I was told my whole life what I couldn't do and what I couldn't have—it was ingrained in my house that success was for other people, not us. I thought when I left home that mentality would change. No, it was everywhere I went. It followed me into the ministry. It still comes up today, but now I see it for what it really is.

When people tell you what you can't do or have, what they are really revealing to you is their own personal belief limitations. They are telling you what *they* don't believe that *they* can have or do. They are throwing their own fears. They are trying to bounce their own limitations off of you. Because even the idea of you succeeding shines a big light onto their belief system, and so it's in their best interest for you not to succeed!

Let me help you out and say this: Succeed anyway. Use your faith anyway. This is your life, and it's God's plan for you, so it's time to throw that old junk off. Get it out of your mind. That's their story. That's not your story.

I don't care how much you have heard their lies—don't believe the lies. God is limitless. He's pure energy and love. He made you in His image, and put you in a body and on this earth for a reason. Part of being a believer is tapping into His divinity within the context of your own life and living out your true story. That story is what He says about you, and not what other people say about you.

You can choose to believe all the negative things people have said, or you can choose to believe what God says. If you believe what they say, you'll stay the same and keep repeating the same old story! To advance is to break free from the cage of fear and break free from what others have told you that you can and cannot do. To advance is to walk in the light of what God has said and has put on your heart for your own life.

It takes a fierce reality check to say "NO" to the lies and limitations of others about your own life. It takes a brave commitment—a daily choice sometimes—to throw off the opinions of others and, instead, choose God's opinion of you. God's opinion will always advance you in one way or another. People are fickle. Sometimes you'll hear wonderful things from them and other times you won't. Choose God's opinion.

It is an effort, but a wonderful effort, to adopt God's perspective and start seeing yourself for who you really are. You are a child of God—a whole and eternal being who is here to grow, experience life, increase, overcome, and ADVANCE in all areas. So, choose to be limitless and stop telling yourself lies about what is possible.

You serve a limitless and "all things are possible" God. And again, you are His child and made in His image. YOU are capable of advancing more than you ever dreamed possible. Give yourself the luxury of dreaming, of taking off the limits, and having faith in God and your own life's possibilities. Because whatever God has put on your heart to do is more than just possible—it's doable!

CHAPTER 7

Create Your Atmosphere with Your Mouth

I don't want to ask God for what I need—His Word already told me that He will supply all my needs according to His riches in Glory (Philippians 4:19). So, I tell Him what I want. I aim my thoughts and my words higher. Why? Because I want to go beyond just getting needs met. I know that obtaining "wants" destroys "needs." This is why I aim for my dreams, my destiny, and the big things I want.

It's Not Greed, It's Growth

This economic world is a dark place, and a believer can make a bigger dent in the darkness by being successful. Your financial abundance isn't just about the power to purchase things, but also the power to bless people and fund the good things that matter. Being a light in a dark place is a wonderful thing! Blessing others is a wonderful thing!

But if you are consumed by your own needs all the time and living in a mental state of lack, you won't have very much energy to even think about how to impact the world because your focus will be so much on just meeting your need. Think about it: Have you ever noticed how when you are really hungry you don't immediately think about offering others a bite of your food?

When my wife, Cathy, and I eat out at a restaurant, if she is starving, she doesn't even think to offer me a bite! Well, at least not until she's got some of that food in her stomach. Suddenly, she will stop, take a breath, and say, "Jesse, do you want a bite?" I think, *Yeah, woman, I want a bite!* I wanted a bite the moment that plate hit the table.

Now, why does she wait to ask me? She waits because when you're starving, it's hard to think past the hunger—the brain silently screams at you "EAT!" Then, you hit a point where the stomach and brain relax because they aren't consumed with yourself.

Never forget that need is lower than desires. Do I have needs? Not anymore because my wants took care of them. I know some people think this sounds cocky and arrogant—but it's not. It's about focusing my faith higher. It's about speaking what I want, not what I have. It's about creating my atmosphere with my mouth, and I do it both when I pray and when I live out my day.

I can do what God said I could do. I can have what God said I could have. And you can, too. Don't get stuck just thinking about needs. Think higher. Create an atmosphere of abundance with your mouth—because that is one channel through which advancement flows.

Don't Cancel Out Your Prayers— Fill Your Atmosphere with Words that Speak the Answer

You can't speak like that old song says, "Gloom, despair, and agony on me! Deep, dark depression, excessive misery..." and expect to feel anything good or better!

You can't speak lack all the time and expect abundance. You charge your atmosphere with faith in God for what you want, by praying for what you want, and speaking what you want.

It's a waste of spiritual energy to pray for the positive but speak what's negative—it's like cancelling out your prayers. Why bother doing that? If you are going to pray in the morning, don't cancel your prayers out throughout the day. Don't waste your breath or your spiritual energy on what you don't want to come to you.

Talking about the problem all the time just exacerbates the problem in your own mind. If you do that, you are just giving that problem more energy to keep perpetuating itself—in fact, you are having faith in the problem. You're calling it in! I like to say that if I focus on my priorities, it eliminates my confusion—I focus on the solution, not the problem. So, if you like where you are, keep talking about where you are. But if you want to do something different, you've got to think and talk differently.

Change your atmosphere with words that matter. Fill your atmosphere with words that speak the answer—which may be the Word of God, or your end goal. Again, say what you want. Don't bother with saying what you have. Because everything in this life is energy, and with God, all things are possible, which means circumstances are subject to change (2 Corinthians 4:18).

Good Things are for You—
Faith and Patience are Required to Receive from God

Patience is a fruit of the Spirit for a reason—it's part of the nature of God in you, and you need it to inherit the promises of God (Galatians 5:22-23). The more you dwell in the Holy Spirit and sow to the spirit, the more of His Spirit rubs off on you. Some things take more time than others, and so patience is required. Remember that you are eternal. Don't let "time" become overly stressful to you. You are going to live forever.

I don't bend to the pressure of time. Yes, I'd like my manifestations yesterday, who wouldn't? But I've gotten to the point in my life where I realize that time itself has no bearing on my blessings and miracles—I will receive, and time makes no difference. I'm going to live forever. I get it here or I get it there, but I put my faith toward the here and now anyway. That's why it's easier for me to exercise patience when I'm believing for something by faith—I've let go of the pressure of time.

A delay is not a denial. We may not even see the bigger picture when it comes to what we ask God for in this life—but we can still ask! In looking back at my own life, I can see that sometimes I've asked for things I wasn't mature enough and prepared to handle. All of us do this from time to time. We might ask for things that God knows we can't handle, but we still have the free will to ask, and we have the joy of imagining the day when it arrives.

For instance, a three-year-old little boy can ask for a big motorcycle. He can ask, but he couldn't handle it if he got it. But as he grows, if he keeps his mind on that bike, he can train and become a motocross champion by the time he is 16 years old. Sometimes your faith will bring you things quickly, and sometimes you have to grow in order to receive what you want—that means growing mentally and spiritually so that you can handle it.

"But let patience have her perfect work, that ye may be perfect and entire, wanting nothing" (James 1:4)—let patience have her perfect or "maturing" work. You are growing every time you exercise patience with your faith.

Remember that *"The young lions do lack, and suffer hunger: but they that seek the LORD shall not want any good thing"* (Psalm 34:10). Good things are for you. God wants that—but you have to seek Him, you have to put faith in Him, and you have to use the words of your own mouth to create your atmosphere.

People have all kinds of differing opinions about what you should have or should do—but they aren't you. They may not have the same desires. They surely don't have the same passion. That's ok. Let their words roll off of you like water on a duck's back. Don't let other people's negative words about what you are believing for seep into your mind—don't let them kill your dream or steal your joy.

I don't care what they say, your faith can move mountains. But you are going to have to "say to the mountain." What you are believing for must not only be in your mind but in your mouth. Like Jesus said in Mark 11:23, *"For verily I say unto you, That whosoever shall say unto this mountain, Be thou removed, and be thou cast into the sea; and shall not doubt in his heart, but shall believe that those things which he saith shall come to pass; he shall have whatsoever he saith."*

God wants the best for you. Do you want the best for you, too? If you haven't been on your own side in a while, today is the day to change. Today! Do it now. Make a quality decision that every time that old story of what you can and can't do rises up in your head, you will change that story. "I can't do that because...." will become "I can do all things through Christ who gives me strength!" (Philippians 4:13).

Get into the habit of "saying" to your mountain. I like to command my mountains! I command what I want to come into my life to come, in Jesus' name. And I command what I want to get out of my life to go, in Jesus' name.

Life is Always About Transition— There is No Such Thing As "I've Arrived"

Life is always moving forward. This means that transition is part of life—in fact, it's a constant. Nothing stays the same. So, there is no such thing as "I've arrived." Instead, it is more like, "I'll always be growing and advancing in my life. God will encourage me and challenge me. He will always have more for me to say and do." Once you know this, you can relax as you move in faith knowing that this is the way life works.

The goal of a Christian should always be to advance—to go forward, never backing up and never giving up. It means that the natural ebb and flow of life may be movement and rest, but when you follow after God, you will always have new challenges and new blessings to look forward to.

Long after you obtain or do what is on your heart today, there will be another reason to use your faith. I don't care how old you are; God will stir you to do or say more for Him and to help others in some way. So, don't look at this as some struggle—it's a blessing! It's the way it is supposed to be—conquering, overcoming, moving forward, walking in love, and living by faith!

Advancement Must Be a Revelation to You— Your Inspiration Will Produce Manifestation

When your own advancement becomes a revelation to you, you will be inspired to draw that revelation into manifestation. If it's not a revelation to you, you will find yourself settling for whatever comes down the pipe in life.

There is a big difference between contentment with life and settling for whatever comes in life. Your desire to live well, to advance in what God's put on your heart and mind, must be a revelation to you—a cause that is worth getting excited about.

When you look at your life, every day, in every little way, train yourself to see the good. Train yourself to pick out the good in other people. Train yourself to pick out the good in the day. If you do, you'll learn to see obstacles that come up a lot differently than the person who is fixated on problems.

You'll be able to see a solution. You'll be able to see an opportunity. You'll be the leader in your own life and the force of faith in God within you will rise up to meet the challenge—but only if your goal is advancing. Make advancing your goal.

Let the idea of advancing come up and out of your spirit and go through your soul—your mind, will, and emotions—so that you can take the steps necessary with your own natural body.

When Your Faith is Activated, Advancement Runs Toward You

A lot of believers have stopped believing. They are going to Heaven, but other than that, they aren't advancing in life. They are stagnant. Their faith in God is actually dormant. It's still in there in seed form, but it's not being watered at all.

Passion is lost when we let our faith go dormant. Humdrum lives are not what God intended for us when He created this beautiful planet. We are powerhouses walking around like wilting flowers! We all have destinies housed inside of us that we won't often even look at—we get caught up with daily things and ignore ourselves. God gave each of us a life, and that life is meant to be lived right here and right now.

Right where you are is the perfect place to start, even if it looks like it's the worst place to start. God is known for showing up when we show up for ourselves. Faith activated causes advancement to run toward us. Fear activated causes advancement to run away from us. We have not been given a spirit of fear! We have been given a spirit of love, power, and a sound mind (2 Timothy 1:7).

Fear runs headlong against your advancement. I hear so many Christians say things like, "You believe in that faith stuff? I tried that..." The truth is that "trying" doesn't get much of anything done. Faith in God isn't a "try it on" concept. It's a lifestyle that promotes advancement from the spirit, through the soul, and into the body.

You cannot please God without it. The scripture makes that plain (Hebrews 11:6). If you don't have faith, you aren't pleasing God— and you sure aren't living the life you could be living. Dreaming is wonderful! Vision is wonderful! There is passion and freedom in a person who believes that God has given them the power and inner tools necessary for the purpose He has placed in their life.

Your natural mind wants to protect you from the adventure of living by faith and going after your dreams. Fear is a natural state of being for so many people, but it literally cuts you off from your own potential. That's because you have a natural mind and not a faith mind. You have to renew your mind if you want a faith mind. And still, your natural mind will try and dominate you.

Once you recognize and accept that fear rising is going to contaminate your faith and stunt your future growth, it's easier to notice when it arises and determine that fearing is NOT in your best interest. It's not your best state of being. You can hear the fearful thoughts rise up, and even feel them try and steer you—and this is when you must hit your internal pause button and choose something different.

This is when you speak God's Word. This is when you say what you want and not what you have. Pray if you need to, but this is when you do like Jesus and start "saying" to your mountain (Mark 11:23).

Notice Jesus never "prayed to the mountain"—He spoke! Speak what aligns with what you actually want.

You can't put God on the backburner, give Him one day a week, and expect to see your faith in Him soar. If you want to advance spiritually, faith is something you use on a daily basis, not a Sunday basis. The same is true with your natural body or your finances. It's what you think, say, and do on a daily basis that matters even in the natural. It matters even more in the spiritual! And what you want is to have both of those areas working for you, not against you.

The world and the devil will try to work against you—but if you and God are working together, nothing can stop you in the end. You may be delayed, but you will not be denied. You may have obstacles, but you will overcome. You may see a no-win scenario with your eyes, but your faith will produce a win-win scenario. You are eternal. It's not over till it's over, and it ain't ever going to be over! You win just by default because you are God's own and are going to live forever, but you can also win right here on earth. Don't settle!

You advance through your agreement with the Word of God—nothing trumps that, not even what you dream up to say—so make sure the Word of God is above even your own word. Fold your own word into the Word. Put yourself in the scripture. Like I showed you earlier, I put my name in there when I'm confessing it so that I personalize the good thoughts God has about me and for me. I suggest the same to you.

When sickness hits your body, don't deny it—and don't settle for it. I've heard people say, "I got the flu. I guess I'm going to have a week of this flu." Look, it's a blessing of God that we've got medicine and drugs to help us recover from things, but our own mind also works to promote health in our body. We can give up and settle, or we can speak up, think up, and pray and help the mess go away sooner. We can act on our own best interests, or we can act on the sickness' best interest.

Personally, if something tries to attack me, like the flu, I fight back with my mind and my mouth. The Word immediately rises up in me, and I speak for up my own health. I don't deny the sickness. That's dumb. I deny its right to remain by focusing on God's promises.

With my mouth, I speak Word-based things over myself like, "I am the healed, not the sick! God restores health to my body! Jesus went to the cross and by the stripes they laid on His back, I was healed—"am sick" has to bow to "was healed!" Glory! No weapon formed against me shall prosper!" (1 Peter 2:24; Isaiah 54:17)

I also back that up with actions that work with my body—because I know my body. I've lived long enough in it to know that when something is fighting me, prayer helps my mind, confession builds my faith, and exercise itself helps my body to shake things off. So, I get on the treadmill, and sometimes I speak to myself the whole time! I tell my body what it's going to do.

When I eat, I don't clog up my system with junk when it's trying to fight—I do my best in that area so that I can give my body something to work with. Then, I sleep! Now, that's what I do. You must do what you know to do in the natural—but never settle for just the natural. Use your spirit and your soul, too. You are a whole being, and sometimes it takes the whole being to be healed.

Remember, the Word says that everything named has to bow at the name of Jesus—so you can use the name of Jesus over whatever illness, problem, or circumstance that has a name (Philippians 2:9-10). Speak the solution. Remember the cross and the stripes laid on Jesus' back for your healing. Run toward your advancement in health with faith, words, and actions that support what you want—not what you have!

Don't be one of those people who settles for sickness and just accepts it naturally. And especially don't be one of those people who claims they are believing for their complete and total health in Jesus' name while they are sick in bed eating a two-ton can of nacho cheese and chasing it with a gallon of orange soda. Work with yourself, spiritually and physically, or you just might meet Jesus early—and with cheese dripping out your mouth.

CHAPTER 8

Honor the Ebb and Flow of Life

I'm inspired about the ministry God has given me. I have not lost the passion of preaching the Gospel, and I've been preaching for over 40 years at the time of this book. I'm still passionate and joyful, but those things don't come from outside—they are generated from the Spirit of God living in me as I move forward from faith to faith.

People look at me and say, "Brother Jesse, when are you going to retire?" I laugh inside myself at that because what am I going to do? Fish? Play golf? Sit around watching the world go by? There is nothing wrong with fishing, golfing, or relaxing and watching the world go by—but if that's all I'm looking forward to in this life, I won't last very long! I need much more.

I'm not a man of hobbies. I'm interested in the work of God and accomplishing what I'm here to accomplish. It brings me joy to have fulfillment in God's plan. I live for something greater than myself, and so I don't spend time just wishing I was somewhere else.

I enjoy what I do, and I see no need to ever stop doing it. Especially not to just sit around on a beach somewhere getting burnt, or on a golf course fighting back the want to cuss because the ball won't go where I want it to go!

If all you are looking to do is get out of your own life, you are missing it—because you should be enjoying your days and living as unto the Lord every day. Passion isn't something you need to drum up. It's something already inside of you that needs to be lit up.

If you haven't been living with any joy, let me tell you that joy is not going to come from outside of you and light your fire. You'll retire and get on that golf course and have fun for a while, but you won't be joyful for long. In fact, you probably will need a golf cart because you'll get worn out just walking the course!

But if you understand that you have command over your body, and you can use your mind and your mouth to stay in line with your spirit, then you will age a whole lot better. Abraham had purpose, and at 100 years old, he got his wife pregnant—that's a man with vision! Now, you may not want that to happen, but that can happen because anything is possible with God, faith, and passion!

The Ebb and Flow of Advancing— A Time to Move, a Time to Rest… So You Can Move Again!

Think about it. Have you ever seen someone who works all their life only to retire and end up lethargic and stagnant after a few years in? The joy they looked forward to experiencing seems to wane, and some people even end up sick or dying when they were healthy before. Why? Because we need purpose in life—we need to grow and we need something to look forward to.

Never fall into the trap of thinking that "the good life" is sitting around doing nothing day after day. That is not going to fulfill your

70

heart in the long run because God did not create you to be lethargic or stagnant. You were created to grow.

For some people, the idea of always transitioning and always advancing seems difficult to accept, but it is a fact of life, and once you accept it, you can begin to relax into it instead of trying to make it stop. You cannot stop time or transitions. Nothing stays the same. Life is always changing—sometimes bit by bit and other times leap by leap!

So, to be challenged and grow as a result is actually a blessing. Rest is wonderful. So is retirement, for some. But if you take it too far, eventually boredom sets in. To keep life interesting and to keep our mind and body healthy, we have to move.

If you are constantly looking to stop moving, it's probably because you have not given yourself mental and physical rest. Energy comes out of a rested mind and body. Advancing requires both rest and movement, and most of all, it requires that you conquer fear. If you fear rest, don't—it isn't forever. It's a portion of time. And no matter how good you think you're doing, if you don't rest, you aren't doing as well as you think. You simply can't perform your best without rest.

The feeling of being overwhelmed, poorly made decisions, and bad choices in life often come either from an unrested mind and body, or a mind plagued by fear. The offshoots of fear are things like overthinking, worry, and anxiety. All things that can steal your rest. But there is rest in God. Choosing to live by faith is good for your body because stress is a killer. There is peace in faith!

What drives out fear? The Word says it is love—a perfect love—that casts out all fear (1 John 4:18). When you live by faith, you are saying that you know God loves you so much that He will perform His Word in your life. You are saying that you believe it to such a degree that you can put your head down on the pillow and rest knowing that God is with you—you've done all you know to do, and He will take over from there.

If fear is getting in your way, I encourage you to focus on the perfection of God's love for you. Do a study on it. Meditate on it. Confess His love over your life. Use scriptures. Speak them. Shift your thoughts to them whenever the fearful thoughts come. Let them take over.

You want to be saturated in the knowledge of the love of God when you are combating a mind that wants to fear. Because knowledge of God's love on a deeper level helps you let those fears go so you can rest your mind when you need to, and then get up and move on to what you need or want to do again!

Don't Cheat Your Future by Stealing from Today

Now, I know some people are like I am—I'm always interested in movement and at one time in my life, resting was difficult for me to do. There was a time in my ministry and in my life that I thought that I didn't need rest. I thought downtime was a waste of time. I figured I'd succeed more if I could cut out that rest junk. Wrong!

Even Jesus Christ rested. He rested in the boat on the way to the other side of the sea of Galilee with His disciples—Jesus slept so well that a storm was raging and they had to wake Him up to tell Him. Jesus took times of rest in the wilderness, too. He had alone time with God. He fasted, prayed, and rested.

Do you think that when Jesus was in that wilderness by Himself that there were people in town that could have used His preaching and miracle working power? Do you think they could have found something for Him to do, somewhere for Him to go, and someone for Him to minister to? Of course. Sure. Definitely! But even Jesus Himself knew the rest He needed was necessary for Him to fulfill His destiny as Savior of the world—so if Jesus Himself needed rest, you do, too. If He took it, even though He could have been doing something else that others thought of as more "productive," then you

CHAPTER 9

You Have a Journey of Faith: To Advance, You Must Let Go of the Past

You are going somewhere—and what lies at the end of it all is nothing short of VICTORY. You may or may not remember the lyrics to that old Gospel hymn, "Victory in Jesus" but I want to share them with you now.

They are: "O victory in Jesus, my Savior, forever. He sought me and bought me with His redeeming blood; He loved me ere I knew Him, and all my love is due Him, He plunged me to victory beneath the cleansing flood. I heard about His healing, of His cleansing pow'r revealing. How He made the lame to walk again and caused the blind to see; and then I cried 'Dear Jesus, come and heal my broken spirit,' and somehow Jesus came and bro't to me the victory. I heard about a mansion He has built for me in Glory. And I heard about the streets of gold beyond the crystal sea; about the angels singing, and the old redemption story, and some sweet day I'll sing up there the song of victory." (E.M. Bartlett, 1939)

It blesses me, even though it's very old, but I must say that I don't believe that we have to wait until "some sweet day" to experience and sing the song of victory. Jesus went to the cross to give us victory in the here and now, and not just the forever after.

But what I like about this song is that it's about taking a journey—a journey to victory that is possible because of the cleansing flood of our redemption through Jesus' shed blood. We are plunged into victory because of what He did—and it's now our job to walk in it and enjoy it, and live by faith in His glorious work on the cross.

All our love is due Him. We really do have victory in Jesus. So, I must say it again: You are going somewhere. You have something to attain. You have a destiny to complete. And to get there, you often will have to let go of some things in order to move forward in God's plan for your life.

Abraham's Journey of Faith

I want to share a little about Abraham now because if anybody had to leave the past behind him in order to receive his prize, Abraham did. Genesis 12:1 says, *"Now the Lord said unto Abram, Get thee out of thy country, and from thy kindred, and from thy father's house, unto a land that I will shew thee."* Notice something in that verse— notice that a journey is beginning here. I call it "the journey of faith" because that's exactly what it is. God is the architect of our lives. And we live our best life when we follow His plans. It is a journey that requires faith.

Leaving his own country, his extended family, and his father's house was no small feat for Abraham—very, very few of us will be required to take such drastic measures. But all of us, I can tell you, will be required to break from the past in some way. If we only look at where we've been, we cannot see where we should go.

As Paul said, we can't press toward the mark without letting go. Because the very act of pressing forward to what's ahead requires that we get in the habit of forgetting what's behind. So, there will be things you must leave in the past—you likely already know what they are. Old thoughts, old habits, old ways, and perhaps there will be some people, too.

God will make our journey fruitful but only in proportion to our faith. If we want greatness in our lives, we will have to train ourselves to have faith in God's promises. So, look back at Abraham. If you keep reading Genesis 12:2-3, you'll see that God made him some promises. You are linked up with those promises. How? Galatians 3:29 tells us that in Jesus, because of what He did on the cross, we have become the "seed of Abraham" and that makes us *"heirs according to the promise."*

Abraham was promised (1) land (2) seed, and (3) a blessing. Think of it like this. His promises are yours because, now, you're in the family. This means you are spiritually linked to the Father of Faith, Abraham, through Jesus Christ regardless of your nationality, your skin color, or your culture. You are blessed. Notice what Abraham got and realize that you are meant to have this as well.

Land represents a place of your own. Seed represents physical and/or spiritual children. A blessing represents God's hand of abundance on your life, your labor, and your family. These are all areas that God chose as advancements for Abraham, but he had to let go in order to receive God's promise. None of it dropped out of the sky.

Now, back up and remember that Abraham was asked to take a journey to a land that God promised to show him. He didn't know yet where he was to go. He stepped out in faith, not knowing yet the end result of that action. Even more mind-blowing is that God didn't promise to give him that land! He just told him to go. He didn't say He'd do anything else. God just said that He wanted to show him something. So, Abraham had to just trust that God had his best interest at heart.

What does this tell us? It tells us that every one of us must learn to walk by faith and not by sight (2 Corinthians 5:7). On Abraham's journey to the Promised Land, he would come to develop a much closer communion with God—that communion would lead him to break with his past. If you want to advance, you must realize that the journey of faith requires that you break from the past.

You must become singular, which means you have to realize that it's you and God alone in this journey of faith. People may come and go in your life, or they may stay forever. Regardless of others, only you and God will walk your journey of faith. Your Mama cannot live your journey for you. Neither can your husband, your wife, your pastor, your best friend, or any other person. Your journey of faith is your own, and it's personal.

It's you and God! And God requires faithfulness to Him and Him alone—and that is why He wants no other gods before Him, no other things above Him, and no one in your life taking His rightful place as God (Exodus 20:3). They may be with you in support or not, but just know this: God is with you and He has some amazing things to show you, if you will walk with Him in faith.

Sometimes we may start to feel lonely on the journey. We may be tempted to cling to our past or to people—we may be tempted to put other things above God because the journey of faith isn't always comfortable. The truth that we must know is this: We are never alone. God promised to never leave or forsake us (Hebrews 13:5). And nothing that we try to put in God's place will ever satisfy us for long or advance us in the journey He has called us to walk.

It's going to take a quality decision on your part to leave what's behind you in the past where it belongs. Don't put anything above Him. It'll help you to advance in your journey if you keep reminding yourself that God loves you, and that advancing in the journey itself will require you to have faith in Him. Remind yourself that He will never leave you or forsake you. He has promised that He is with you, and He always will be—every single step of the way, for the entire journey.

You Have a Divine Right to Run Your Race

I want to warn you. When you are believing for big things or even small things, there are people who might not want to see you succeed—every good word you say or change you make causes them to feel a little fear. Your success becomes a mirror to their choice to stay the same. They may try and strip you of your inspiration, your confidence, and even lash out at you just to try and hold you back. Don't let them.

Don't let another person's insecurity and fear become yours. They have their own life to live—and they don't have a right to steal the dreams, desires, and destiny that are in your heart. You protect your own heart when you realize that what they say and do against you isn't really about you at all. It's about them. Just knowing that helps you to let their words roll off your back so that you can stay the course.

You have a race to run. If you want to get there, the naysayers need to take a backseat in your own mind. You can love them. You can appreciate them in many ways. But you should not give your power to them. You have a divine right to own your own dreams, desires, and destiny. Nobody has the power to steal your confidence in God or yourself unless you let them. Nobody has the power to take your faith, your purpose, or your destiny. Don't let them!

You have power over yourself—and with God, you can accomplish what you want to accomplish. You can have what you want to have. Your future is too important to give up just because somebody dismisses it—because you are designed by God to be a mover, a shaker, a sower, and a grower. Beware that your candlestick not be removed (Revelation 2:5).

Let them balk. Don't even try and change them. You'll just be wasting breath and time. You have pearls inside—a valuable purpose. Don't cast your pearls before people who don't value who you are, what you want, or where you are going in life (Matthew 7:6). They'll just trample what you value because they don't value it. Keep moving forward with faith in God and in yourself.

We Get What We Believe For

When I was young and going into the ministry, almost everybody in my sphere cut me down for desiring to preach the Gospel. They didn't believe in me, so they sure didn't encourage me. In fact, my own pastor told me I shouldn't preach.

I was constantly warned about how hard it was going to be and how much I needed to "watch it" because I was just about to get my can kicked from one end of life to the other. As I write this book, I'm celebrating 40 years of ministry, and it was unbelievable to many back then, but it wasn't to me! That's why I am where I am today. I never believed for misery. I never believed for failure. I chose what I knew God had told me to do, and I did it. It was not always easy, by no means, but I had faith that God would take care of it all if I did my part. And He has!

God is still using me. He is still stretching my faith. I'm doing more now than I did back then. I'm still running my race in faith long after the people who discounted me have retired from their own hard road.

You see, we get what we believe for—because what we believe affects the choices we make and the faith we use. What we believe affects every decision we make. It affects whether we settle for something or move forward and stretch ourselves. What we believe affects everything!

So, when people told me how rough my future was going to be, I just smiled—because I knew what I believed trumped what they assumed would happen. "What if it all goes bad?" should be countered inside of yourself with, "What if it all goes great?" I knew that they couldn't receive my ministry because they weren't thinking like God. He can use anyone, and often uses people nobody thought could or should be used!

You Are Under No Obligation to Have Faith in the Naysayers— You Will Succeed as You Obey and Have Faith in God and Yourself

You see, I knew that the Word said, *"Be ye therefore followers of God, as dear children"* (Ephesians 5:1). Other Bible translations use the word "imitators" instead of "followers" making it even more distinct. But I want you to notice the Word doesn't say, "Be ye therefore followers of the naysayers." Let me take it even further: It doesn't even say, "Be ye therefore imitators of the first Church." Now, stay with me here—don't get offended!

The first Church went through a lot of persecution. Do you know why? They were cutting the path and they did not even have the written Word yet. And they were in Jerusalem! What were they doing in Jerusalem when Jesus expressly told them to go into the world and preach the Gospel? They stayed in Jerusalem ten years.

Had they obeyed Jesus to the letter, they wouldn't have even been there to get persecuted. Nero wouldn't have had to kill any of them because they wouldn't have been there. Have you ever thought about that? The Word says that obedience is better than sacrifice—because it is (1 Samuel 15:22). You can avoid a lot of trouble just by obeying the Word. You can do wonderful things whether you obey the Word or not, but your best life will always be linked to your obedience.

Jesus didn't trash-talk His own vision. He didn't complain about how hard everything was going to be for Him in ministry. We never hear Jesus pleading with the people and saying, "I tell you what, if I don't hear from you today, if you don't bless My ministry, we can't go to Capernaum!" We never read about Jesus saying, "Things are so tough, I can't even go back home to see Mama! I need a new robe and some sandals, people. I'm tired of eating fish! I want to do so much, but it's all sooooo hard, won'tcha help Me?!" No!

Jesus imitated His Father. He knew how to pray. He had faith. He moved in faith, and rested Himself when necessary so that He could go back out and DO what God sent Him to do. Jesus did not cut down or doubt His own vision, and He is our example.

So, I don't care if the person you look up to the most cuts your vision down—they aren't Jesus. Even if the person you love the most can't see what you see—they aren't Jesus. God has your back. If He told you to do something, if He birthed it into your spirit, then it will fire you up—you'll be lit from within to do it.

Have faith in God. You are under no obligation to have faith in those who cut down your vision, purpose, or whatever it is that you are believing God for in your own life. So, don't let them distract you. "Focus" isn't just a word—it's a mandate for advancement.

CHAPTER 10

"Focus" Isn't Just a Word— It's a Mandate for Advancement

Distractions are dangerous to your advancement—if you let them become a main attraction, they'll steal your future from you, one little bit at a time. Advancing is about what you let go of just as much as what you move toward. You cannot fill your day and your life with distractions and expect to go where you want. Yes, there are things you have to do, but they don't have to be your focus. Your focus should be your priority—and you must let go of the distractions that keep you from it.

I've been offered a lot of good opportunities in my life that I chose not to take because they didn't align with my priorities. They looked good, sounded good, and even seemed good, but they were not in line with what God told me to do. They were definitely not in line with who God called me to be.

You see, your decisions should line up with who you are called to "be." You can't separate "being" from all your "doing" if you want to advance and fulfill your destiny. If you do, you won't go in the direction that is right for you.

A lot of people look at what I have today and consider me to be a man of substance—but the truth is that I was "a man of substance" before I had anything that they could see. My vision has always been within my being. I am the owner of it, and it was seeded in me long ago. It became what I thought about, what I said, and it helped me to align with what I did—which, in turn, manifested into what I have come to see with my own eyes. I saw it long ago. "Focus" is what I had to do to stay on target with what was seeded into me.

"Focus" isn't just a word—it's a mandate for advancement. Distractions come and go—and you are in control of how long you let them stay. Dreamers can't see their dreams come to pass if they let every whim of distraction steal their mind-space. You'll lose the years one day at a time if you let distractions take over. Ask yourself if what you are doing on a daily basis fits the dream you have for your life. Ask yourself if what you are focusing on fits with the person you want to be. Ask yourself if what you're doing is helping or hindering your vision.

It's easier to say no to some things when you value your future and who you want to be. Yes, you'll disappoint some people. Some will think you're crazy. One day, they'll see your vision or dream take place, and they won't think you were so crazy back when you were taking control over distractions. But even if they do think that forever, does it matter? They aren't living your life. They don't have your desires. God gave them their own life and their own desires, their own destiny—don't expect everybody to be happy when you choose to follow your own! They might not understand, and maybe they aren't even meant to understand. You are meant to understand! Because it's for you!

Don't focus on where you've been. Don't focus on where you are. Focus on where you're going. Then, discipline yourself to go there—to be the person God has called you to be. If He's called you to be bold, you are meant to be bold. God has put the attributes you need to fulfill your vision within your very personality. You have what it takes! With Him, you can do anything.

I have friends who say, "Jesse believes the most unbelievable and impossible things!" Oh yeah, I do. I let myself dream big—because the capacity to dream big is in me. A lot of people don't even let themselves dream. They don't even take the time to see what God puts on their heart. They don't let Him bring up what really matters to them.

God will support you in the vision He gives you. You have to allow yourself the freedom to dream—not just about what you want to do, but who He has created you to be. I do a lot of things, but who I am is foundational to all those things. I'm going to be me throughout eternity! So are you! So, you might as well let yourself out of the bag and start living as the person you really are inside, and not who others tell you are or who others want you to be.

If I would have listened to what other people wanted for me, I never would have lived with much joy, and I wouldn't have accomplished anything for the Lord. It's His good pleasure to see His children advancing in who they are—right here in the world and in the life He's given us. All of us have something we can do. Be brave enough to allow yourself time and energy to pray and open up to God. Use the imagination He gave you to dream. Get a vision for what you want, what comes up in your spirit, and then decide that no distraction is worth giving it up.

Whether it is spiritual, physical, financial, emotional, or in your relationships—decide now that you aren't going to waste your life wishing and hoping for something God has given you a desire to do, or to have in this life. Faith is available to draw you and your vision together. Say no to the optional things of life that don't support that vision. Don't fill your to-do list with things that don't really matter to you. Focus is a mandate!

Faith Brings Peace—It Does Not Bring Stress Pressure Comes When You Try to Do God's Job

Some of the financial goals I have in order to see the ministry reach more people and change more lives around the world seem outrageous and too big for some people to believe. It's OK. It's not for them. I always want as many people believing with me as possible because the more people using their faith for the project to come to pass, the more powerful and quick the manifestation will be. More faith equals more power to pull things out of the faith zone and into reality.

People question me about how this or that big financial goal is going to happen—the truth is, I don't know how it's going to happen, and it's not my job to figure out completely all the hows in fulfilling a vision. I don't care because God is the One Who gave these goals to me.

There is a lost and dying world of people out there that needs to hear about Christ and the good life that they can live when they are connected to the Lord. So, if it's God's vision, then God is paying for it. He didn't ask me to pay for it; He asked me to believe Him for it! That means the pressure is off of me.

If God is in it, it's doable! If I believe, my faith makes it possible! You see, so many Christians don't advance because they can't think their way around the vision God has given them. They take on the responsibility for making it happen. In reality, God gave it to them so that HE could make it happen! He wants a willing partner. He wants you to live the adventure of trusting Him. He wants to see you soar in life—and break free of the fear the devil would use to hold you back in a humdrum life you don't even like.

God wants you to love your life, and you can't even love it if you don't fill up with His Spirit and follow Him in faith. If you negate His power and try to do it all on your own, the vision will weigh you down, and your mind will be riddled with thoughts about what you cannot do. Stop! Remind yourself Who God is—and pray to Him and speak the Word again over that vision.

You see, we've been taught to "pay" instead of believe Jesus. Let me help you here: If you can do it all on your own, you don't even need God. When God gives you a vision that requires His huge help to get it done, then it requires His help to get it done!

Stop inserting yourself as the responsible party in the visions of God. You pray. You believe. You say and do everything you can in the natural—and then you keep believing that His supernatural will come and overtake your natural. In other words, He will make it happen.

Your job is to believe that God can do His job. Stop trying to take on God's job. That's how you stress yourself out. You can only do what you can do—but faith in God is something anybody can do. We've all been given the measure of faith (Romans 12:3).

You're going to be amazed at what happens when you refuse to give up on your faith. Everything I've done and everything I have today manifested because I refused to give up on my faith in God when I hit the end of what I could do on my own.

I'm not under pressure. I don't live in stress. Why? I decided long ago that I can't do God's job, and my faith is a force that draws my destiny right to me. Whether it's advancing spiritually, physically, financially, or in any other way, I've been created by design to advance God's way, and guess what? So have you.

You've Been Created by Design—
People May Change, but the Vision Shouldn't Change

From the very beginning story of man, God has shown us that we are created to be fruitful, to multiply, replenish, and subdue what He has placed within our world (Genesis 1:28). Every single person is created to be fruitful in life—this means always producing. We are each meant to multiply—this means always increasing.

It's God's command that we replenish—this means that whatever is used, we are responsible for replacing, filling and refilling according to use. And lastly, we have been created to subdue—this means if and when things get out of line, we have been given the authority and power to put things back in line with how they should be. God's way!

These commands—be fruitful, multiply, replenish, and subdue— were given to us as life principles, and they also apply to the vision God gave you. We would not be given these commands if we were unable to do them. God has not changed His mind. You can apply them to whatever vision, goal, or dream you have. They are instrumental instructions for life as things pop up along your path. In fact, they are a whole other book!

I've noticed many trends in ministry come and go over the years. I know that people's styles, interests, and ways of acting in the world may change, but God's principles always remain the same—because they are about the heart of man, and they pertain to life and godliness. Jesus is the same, yesterday, today, and forever no matter how much the styles, interests, and focus of Christians change (Hebrews 13:8).

Trends Come and Go in the Church—
Don't Let Them Distract You from God's Vision

Things come. Things go. In the Church, people go through phases of interest. They may focus on one thing in the Word for a while, then they shift to something else. The music changes. The outreaches change. The clothes change. What's accepted and not accepted changes.

I try to let all these things flow by me without thinking very much about them, unless the basic truth of the Word is what's changing— because that cannot change, or people will go off the rails and lose sight of God's original plan for man through Jesus Christ. I notice that most trends either follow what the world is doing at the time or they are linked to a heart issue.

Forty years ago, nobody could wear jeans in church—the focus was on external dress as a way to prove disassociation with the fleshly nature of the world. Of course, the way you dress has nothing to do with purity in and of itself, but that's where the people were focused. I think if Jesus Himself would have walked in those old churches with His long hair, somebody would have had a chat with Him about getting a haircut!

All the little things people accept or don't accept don't matter, really—other than they distract us from the vision. And God's vision for people at a heart level is what really matters. God loves everyone and wants all to know Him. So, my job as a minister is to bring God's message to people. That's the mission. That's the vision. God changed my life and I share His Word so that people can hear and be changed by God, too. It's wonderful!

The vision should never change—even if people's looks and ways change. Again, fifty years ago, you couldn't preach in a short-sleeved shirt. Sixty years ago, when my family moved us from Catholicism to the Pentecostal Church, women were told they were going to hell for wearing makeup or pants! No short sleeves. Somehow armpits were sexy. I often used to say, "If an armpit turns you on, you need God!"

The reality was that those poor women couldn't wear anything considered attractive to a man. They practically had to wear sack-cloth in order to be considered a good woman and holy. Now, men on the other hand were under no such oppression. Men could wear the best fashion of the day, but not women. Why? Lust.

When a man can't control his own lust, he will try to control women in an effort to control himself—even in the Church, maybe especially in the Church! My mother would tell me as a child, "Why don't you like one of the good Christian girls?" I'd say, "I'm going amongst the Philistines, Mama!" Oh, she hated that.

Submit to Authority, Never to Control

Today things are different, but the reality of changing trends continues, and the principle of trying to control others in an effort to control yourself is also still out there. God's vision hasn't changed—and while we might change in our ways, we shouldn't lose sight of Jesus Christ and Him crucified because when we do, we don't do ourselves any good.

Distractions from the truth in the Church become trends that don't really help anybody and often hurt people. Each of us was created by design and given the measure of faith—but none of us were given a measure of control over others. Our own personal choices are just that, choices. To create little factions of people separated by personal choices is the polar opposite of what God wants, which is unity.

I often say that I'll submit to authority, but not to control. God does not want us backbiting and trying to control one another. Reaching people with the message of Jesus is the vision and all the distractions and tit-for-tat control issues can't be allowed to ruin the message.

The world is too important. People are too important. God calls us to love one another, not hurt one another. Distractions that drive a wedge between us just aren't worth it! We've got too much to do and too many people to reach to lose sight of our vision as the Church. Whether it's concerning our individual purpose or our unified purpose as the body of Christ, "focus" isn't just a word—it's a mandate for advancement!

CHAPTER 11

Common Stumbling Blocks to Advancing Financially

Financial abundance. Money. "Things." Most Christians don't have a problem with advancing spiritually, physically, or relationally—but they often hit a wall when it comes to financial advancement. So many people have limitations in their mind about this part of earthly life.

In fact, when you talk about money, you will instantly feel a reaction from people—and by the reaction, you can know whether they have a mindset of fear around abundance in general or not. Money represents power in this world, and so when financial advancement is talked about, you have knee-jerk reactions that will immediately start to kick!

Some immediately rush to judgment and assume that any desire for financial advancement is off-course. They equate the desire for financial advancement with the concept of greed. That's how you know they have fear surrounding finances—and not a fear of money so much as a fear of power and a fear of their own character.

Fear of getting greedy or seeing somebody else get greedy is at the top of some believers' minds. Fear rules them when it comes to finances. They don't trust *themselves* when it comes to money, so they sure won't trust you!

What do they fear? They fear getting out of God's will and being corrupted by what they assume is "too much"—and they assume what is "too much" based on their fear of their own character. In other words, they don't know how they'd handle it if they were unlimited when it comes to finances. They fear they might do what the Word says and forget God once they've become rich.

Follow the Fear, Find the Reason

Is that really fear of money? Abundant blessings? Things? No, they fear their own character. They fear what they'd do under the influence of having "too much" money. So, while it might seem like greed is all they are concerned about, what they are really concerned about is their own heart under the influence of money. They fear the power. They fear what they might actually do if given the chance to do anything. Because they believe that riches and wealth will give them the power to do anything, which it won't, but that's a whole other book!

All that fear of money has nothing to do with money. It has everything to do with trust. Character is king! And few things prove your character more than having abundant riches and power—because you have the opportunity then to see whether you still want or need God in your life.

"But thou shalt remember the LORD thy God: for it is He that giveth thee power to get wealth" (Deuteronomy 8:18). There is a reason why this scripture is in the Word. We wouldn't need to be told to "remember the Lord," if there wasn't a temptation to forget Him!

Do people forget God once they get what they want in life? Yes. Many of them do. And many don't. But for the ones who do, they usually come back once that money destroys their life in some way.

Prosperity destroys a fool (Proverbs 1:32). Prosperity does not destroy the wise—so trust yourself and realize that just because prosperity destroys fools doesn't mean it'll destroy you! Don't be a fool; that's the takeaway.

Build a firm foundation on the wisdom of God's Word. Build your relationship with Jesus so that it is foundational to your daily life. Learn of Him! Lean on Him. Expect abundance to flow and for it to never get in the way of your relationship with God. Because you actually are going to need God even more when you have more in your life to take care of—the responsibilities of blessings become a weighty curse to people who lack wisdom and lack a core spiritual strength in God.

Spiritual advancement is key and foundational because it is your relationship with the Lord and your value for the wisdom in the Word, that will give you the power to choose to keep God in your life, no matter what. Spiritual advancement is what insulates you from the corruption of your own flesh.

Money won't ruin your life unless you let it, so don't let it! Notice if you have fear, anxiety, or apprehension around the subject of money. Ask yourself why. Drill down to your real reason and then get that fear-junk out of your mind! God loves you. God is abundant. So, you can flow in abundance too. God is not greedy. So you don't have to be greedy either. You do not have to be worried about being corrupted by great wealth—all you have to do is keep God and your spiritual development a priority in your life.

Trust God. Trust yourself. Remind yourself that God lives in you, and He's wise—He can handle abundance and power, and because He's guiding you, you can handle it, too.

Is Abundance God's Will?

Some people don't want abundance for a whole other reason—and it's not that they think they'll get greedy or mismanage it, but that God Himself just doesn't value human abundance, period. So many have told me that they honestly believe that God hates it when people have nice things. They believe that poverty is a blessing in some way—though they don't personally want it.

I notice that they seem to think God worries about every little bit of finances they get, as if He's in Heaven wringing His hands every time they have an inkling of desire for more of anything. They think God worries about them having too much, so they worry about having too much, too. They are often very good people who want to please God and remain humble before Him—and by completely cutting out financial abundance from their thought life, they assume God will be happier with them. They think He might even love them more if they experience the pain of poverty and lack. So, of course, they think that God hates nice things. Nothing could be further from the truth!

Think about Heaven and how abundant it is there. Think about how the scriptures deliberately talk about the abundant, rich, and glorious nature of Heaven. If God really worries about His creation having too much money or nice things here on earth, then why would He make streets of gold, a foundation of layered jewels, and pearly gates in Heaven? (Revelation 21:21)

If abundance is only supposed to be a heavenly reward, why would God send His Son, Jesus, to earth to teach mankind to pray that His will be done in earth as it is in Heaven? Because God wants His will done in both places, and The Lord's Prayer, which was given to us by Christ Himself, reveals that to us (Matthew 6:9-13).

Why Lack Can't Be Holy

The Lord's Prayer is a beautiful guide for living life well—and right in the beginning it tells us that God's very name is holy. It doesn't say "Our Father which art in Heaven, poverty be Thy name..." It says, *"Our Father which art in Heaven, hallowed be Thy name..."* (Matthew 6:10).

Holiness is not imparted to us by some human choice to live in physical and financial lack. Holiness is within the name of God. Everything powerful is within the names of God, and do you know how many names He has? So many! Here are some and their shortened descriptions just to give you an idea.

El—Almighty. Elohim—Our Creator. El Shaddai—The All Sufficient, All Bountiful One. Adonai—The Owner of Life and the One Who Gives Gifts. Jehovah—The Eternal, Permanent, Self-Existent One, the Possessor of Eternal Life. Jehovah-Jireh—Our Provider. Jehoh-Rapha—Our Healer. Jehovah-Nissi—Our Banner, the One Who Delivers, Saves and Brings Victory. Jehovah-Mekaddishkhem—Our Sanctifier. Jehovah-Shalom—Our Peace. Jehovah-Tsidkenu—Our Righteousness. Jehovah-Shammah—Our Ever-Present God. Jehovah-Ro'i—Our Shepherd, Our Guide, Companion, and Friend.

Again, these descriptions are just shortened bits to describe God. All the human languages of the world can't scratch the surface of describing Who God is! And each one of His names is holy. Holiness is within everything God is and stands for. "Holiness" has nothing to do with what is external but everything to do with what is internal.

Lack is not holy. God is holy! God isn't lacking in Heaven, and is Heaven a holy place? Yes, it is. Heaven is both abundant and holy. Heaven doesn't use lack as a measuring stick for God's holiness—in fact, it's the opposite! For too long, we have wrongly assumed that lack is somehow equated with holiness, but this is a lie. Holiness is

God, and for us it's a choice to be more like God and let His Spirit flow through us—it's about our state of being.

Never forget that the Father likes nice things. He created them in Heaven and He also created them on the earth. This is a blessing to us, His creation. So, never make an excuse for the blessings of God on this earth or in your own life—and don't be ashamed for liking something nice. If you desire something nice, you are just taking after your Father in Heaven.

After all, the same people who condemn money are still working for money. Let the elevator go to the top! If money is so bad, why is everyone working for it, buying groceries with it, buying clothes with it or sending their kids to college with it? Why would you work for something you think is evil in the first place?

God doesn't mind you having nice things. Religious people might but not God. Greedy people might but not God. People with power issues might but not God. The truth is that God gave us a rich earth full of natural resources and beauty.

If God had a problem with His people having nice things here on earth, why would He fill the planet with such beautiful and useful natural treasures, and then give mankind the ability to create and fashion beautiful, useful, and pleasurable things, too?

Don't blame God for man's inhumanity to man—there's no shortage of wealth or abundance on this planet. But there is a shortage of unity between people. There's also a shortage of love, and a shortage of individuals who are willing to discipline themselves and do what it takes in order to produce what they want. There are a lot of people who love money more than life, and it creates horrific crimes against humanity around the world. God warned us against mixing love and money.

Don't Fall in Love with Money, It Cannot Love You Back

You will run headlong into problems if you give money what it doesn't deserve—your love. Many people love money and don't have a dime. They are off course. As believers, we should NEVER fall in love with money because money doesn't love us back! It can't. It doesn't have that power.

Money isn't the root of all evil—it's the LOVE of money (1 Timothy 6:10). Plenty of people ruin their lives and wreak havoc in the lives of others by making this terrible mistake. Cruelty around the world often continues because of it.

We always assume rich people love money, but all my life I've known people who love money and don't have a dime. Rich, poor, or in between, lovers of money will do just like 1 Timothy 6:10 says and pierce themselves with many sorrows. Why? Because they are loving something that can't love them back.

God sees our heart, and we were not created to love or serve money—we are told not to make it our master or our god. There is only One God, and He's a jealous God. He wants nothing above Him. Nothing!

Your love should be reserved for God and living things. You can enjoy and like things. You can enjoy and like riches, goods, things, and experiences. You can bless others and help others, and be a part of great change by sending the Gospel around the world. But keep your love where it belongs! Give it to God and give it to others.

If you have some kind of worry about where your heart stands with money, things, or anything tangible, just ask yourself why you want it in the first place. Check your motivation. Why you want anything will reveal your heart. Drill down and you'll learn what you are really after, and why.

If you don't like the motivation behind your answers, don't get under condemnation about it—just pray, ask God to help you let that go, and correct your heart quickly. God loves you and His correction is a blessing! God will help you to make sure you don't go wrong. God is not going to guilt you into giving something up; but He will help you to realign with Him as your first love. Then, you can just enjoy the blessings without the weight, again reserving your love only for God and others.

Advancement Is Birthed, Grown, and Honed in Collaboration with God— "Things" Are for Enjoyment, Do Not Use Them for "Heart Work"

Remember the old saying: "God doesn't mind you having things, as long as things don't have you." There's nothing wrong with having "things." In fact, if "things" weren't OK with Jesus, He wouldn't say that all these "things" will be added unto you if you seek Him first (Matthew 6:33).

There is nothing inherently wrong with wealth either. It can be used as a tool for so much good, in your own family and throughout the world. But don't confuse riches with actual joy or peace—those things can only be produced from the inside out. There is no "security" outside of God, no matter how much stuff or money you have.

Most people don't believe that. They think if they just had enough money, they'd be happy. Or if they just had a great looking body, they'd be happy. Or if they just had this, that, or the other "thing" that they want, they'd be happy. That's putting the cart before the horse. It's ridiculous to expect inner peace or joy from an external thing. You can be temporarily happy, but things in and of themselves don't bring lasting happiness—because that is a spiritual thing.

If you think riches will bring you lasting happiness or real security or anything at all like that, you are thinking naturally—and you are in for a sore disappointment. Being rich won't make you happy, but it will sure make you very comfortable in your misery! Riches will give you options. And if you've never had a lot of options, you might confuse options with lasting joy, peace of mind, or real security.

Real and lasting peace, joy, or security comes from your connection to God, your faith in God, your adherence to His principles for living life well—and, of course, doing what you were put on this earth to do. What He has put on your heart to do matters. You are here for a purpose. You were created to advance!

All "things" lose their power to produce excitement after a while. Even the best things wear out. Many will get boring after a while. You'll find you need another "thing" to try and jump-start the joy you were looking for at the beginning. That's not advancing; that's just accumulating.

Don't fear. God will richly give you ALL things to enjoy (1 Timothy 6:17). That's the point of any "thing" God gives you—it's for pure enjoyment. It's for pleasure. It's for use and making life easier and more blessed. But peace of mind, joy, security, and real success? "Things" can't give you that. That's not their purpose. Their purpose is just for enjoyment. You can't expect them to perform the "heart work" that only God and you working together can do.

Advancement is birthed through the connection we make with the Most High God. Advancement is grown out of the relationship we cultivate with Him on a daily basis, sometimes a moment-to-moment basis. Advancement is honed and artfully perfected when we learn God's Word and actually put His principles into practice.

Don't avoid God when it comes to your finances. It's part of your life. True advancement, God's way, is always going to be a collaborative effort between you and God. Press toward your mark with Him, not alone, in all areas—including finances.

A Lack Mentality Never Goes Away on Its Own

Many people have a lack mentality—even after they have enough money. I know it seems weird, but a lack mentality can exist right alongside wealth reality. It doesn't go away on its own.

Do you give in fear, spend in fear, and even receive in fear, thinking it'll never be enough? A lack mentality always seems to include an underlying fear of scarcity. If you don't work on renewing your mind and living by faith in God about money, that scarcity mindset will not just steal your finances, but it'll also rob you of peace—even if you become very rich.

Remember, you may do wonderful things and reach your goals and experience great wealth. You might get everything you want. But if you don't change how you think, you'll still feel a nagging sense of lack and scarcity. Money itself will not satisfy you the way you thought it would, and you'll be sad about it.

The reality is you'll be "a wealthy poor person" because while you may have a lot in the bank, your mind will still think it's on the edge of being poor. Poverty is in the mind first, just like riches are in the mind first. This is why the Word talks so much about renewing your mind.

It's cultivating your inner world in order to rid yourself of the junk that isn't true. If you don't make your mind rich first, you will not enjoy riches much, even if you attain them. That's why the Word says that when the blessing of the Lord is on you and flowing, it brings riches with no sorrow (Proverbs 10:22). We wouldn't need that distinction mentioned if riches didn't oftentimes come with sorrow.

What you should be seeking is the kingdom of God first (Matthew 6:33). God promises that if you seek the kingdom (not Heaven, but the kingdom of God—meaning God's way of doing things and being right), all the things you want will be added to you. This is why the Bible can say something like God gives riches with no sorrow. Because without God, riches can often bring much sorrow!

Generosity Will Always Beat Scarcity

One of the most wonderful actions you can take to combat a scarcity mindset is to give—often and generously. Make giving a lifestyle. Believe for a return on the financial seeds. When you do that, you'll find out that giving is a powerful faith tool that will help you to break free from the old thoughts of "not enough."

Giving sends a faith signal to both your own mind and God in Heaven. It says that you trust that God will always take care of you. When you expect a return, it says that you believe the Word of God—that whatever you sow, you will reap in multiplied amounts. That is a principle of God, and it applies to every single area of life, including finances.

I'm a tither and a giver, and I love doing it. I sow purposefully and I always expect to reap, always! Now, I know a lot of people say you should give but you shouldn't expect anything in return—but that is just man's fear and totally against the Word of God. Over and over in the Word, we find that God promises something in return for those who give. Don't let fear of the outcome cause you to forfeit a return on your seed. Fear kills faith and stunts harvests. Don't accept that fear!

If we can rely on the promises of God in other areas, why is giving off limits? It's not. I have many messages that deal with finances, and I will not go into detail here, but just know this: Giving will help you to release any fear you may have about money. It feels wonderful. You'll help yourself break free, and you'll do that while you are helping others. And I believe the best way to help others on a deep level is to share the Gospel, both personally as well as by funding world evangelism.

Give when you have the opportunity. Do it every opportunity you can, and watch how it starts busting though those barricades that were holding you back. Watch how it always comes back to you, in multiplied amounts, through various sources and ways.

I do it regularly with purpose, and spontaneously, too. Some days I just wake up and decide to have a "giving day" where I look for extra ways to bless people. I might buy people's meals. I might carry more cash and give to various people I meet throughout my day. I enjoy blessing others. I enjoy giving to organizations and to projects others are doing to make a difference in the world. I especially love sowing into churches and ministries who are taking the Gospel around the world.

If I see a need, I give, but I also give just to flat bless people! They don't have to need a thing, I just want to be a blessing and live my life as a generous person. God has been good to me! I'm a wealthy man today, but I've been a giver from the beginning. I gave when I didn't have much, and I believe that's why today I have a lot.

Years ago, I would not go out and eat so that I could give to others. I would cut back at my own house so that I could give to others. I sowed many seeds—in the form of bikes, washers, dryers, sofas, and all kinds of furniture. I sowed equipment, cash, and cars. I sent more missionaries to places than you can shake a stick at! I did whatever I could to make giving a part of my life—and I have not regretted one seed sown. God has totally blown me away with His blessing on my life.

I still give a lot today. My habit hasn't changed—but my amounts have! As I got more, I increased my giving more. I love it. I do not fear scarcity one iota! That is not a part of my mind, it's not in my mouth, and it's not in my life. My faith in God and my generosity blew scarcity right out of my life.

It can happen for you, too. Make giving part of your life and watch how God uses you to not only bless others, but to manifest multiplied blessings right back to you!

CHAPTER 12

We Need to Advance As a Nation: American Society Under Siege

I'm American and I'm very disturbed by what I see happening today. The Church needs to advance because our society is under siege and we don't have to look further than the news to see that we are going the wrong way. I believe that we, as the Church, need to start being more of a solution, at a deeper level than the sound bites we see so many parroting on the news.

Christianity is meant to advance humanity, and that means it's meant to advance society. We have backed up. We've stopped even. And society as a whole keeps sinking deeper and deeper into depravity and tragedy. Yes, I'm talking about mass shootings here in America.

We all know that it wasn't always this way. We all know that people in this country have lived with guns since the beginning, and yet we didn't see this kind of mass murder all the time. It's happening so much that it's becoming commonplace, and everybody wants to know why.

Even believers ask things like, "Why doesn't God stop these things from happening?" Well, what I have to say in this chapter may not make some people happy, but it is my opinion—and since this is my book, here we go!

Who Sets the Standards? We Do.

We. Have. Failed. We, as the Church, have failed in our mission because we've lost sight of the vision of God for humanity. We've lost our identity. We were once the examples of what love and morality looked like—and a safe place for people to find hope in God. We once preached Jesus Christ and Him crucified. We once preached about the cross and how it washed sins away.

A society that believes that "everything goes" and there is no such thing as sin does not believe it needs redemption. That's our failure as the Church. At one time we preached sin so strongly that we broke people down with nothing but rules and regulations without the heart-message. Now we've let the pendulum swing so far to the other side that we are afraid to step on toes, even if those toes are sinking down into misery, heart pain, and mentally depraved states of living.

You see, we fail our own society when we don't love humanity enough to stand for what is right and good for them at a heart level. It bothers me that today's Church seems to crave acceptance by the world more than we value God's truth. This is why you see such a watering down of the message of God. Today, much of the Church acts just like the rest of the world, and the only difference is the label. But Christianity as a label does not set people free. It does not change society. It does nothing but make us feel good as we sit in the pew, while our society is melting down.

We cannot let go of our message just because the world is becoming more godless. We can't expect to advance humanity if we are in league with the same evils that are dragging society back.

We already know that many people don't want God in our schools, they don't want the influence of God in the government, and many just plain don't want Him in their lives at all. They want "God" in a little church on a corner of a back road, with no money in which to do anything, and no influence on society at all whatsoever. That's why they attack the prosperity message so much—it's about power.

The Church today is giving up its power more and more in a spiritual way. We should set the standards for what is right, moral, and pure—yet most churches are more interested in the colored-lights they sing under on Sunday morning than they care about teaching the Bible. And many are more interested in filling up a debt-ridden building by preaching the softest message they can than they are interested in preaching the right, moral, and pure Word of God. Nobody wants to offend anybody. Nobody wants to speak up much. Why? Because the Church is filled with sin just like the world is, and the glass houses, so to speak, already have so many cracks that the preachers often feel too guilty about their own sin and "indiscretions" to say anything about society's!

Our reputation is shot! To the world out there, they believe that they can hardly find a preacher who hasn't committed fraud or adultery. The office of minister and priest has been downgraded so much. It is to the detriment of our society that the trust between people and ministry has been broken.

Who sets the standards? We do. All you have to do is look around to see that the Church is not an influencer in society anymore. And what happens when people don't care about God's ways anymore? What happens when you remove God and morality from society? You get a greater propensity for evil and immorality. You get what you see today.

The Church needs to rebuild its reputation as an anchor in society—and that means we, as believers, cannot say one thing and do another. We cannot lie, cheat, steal, and run around with women and expect to be an anchor for society. We will ruin our own lives and hinder the lives of others in the process.

We cannot think just for "today" and live by every whim while calling ourselves believers. Society depends on us laying and continually laying the foundation for what is right before God. If the backbone loses its strength, how does the body stand? It doesn't. It flounders and wobbles.

Why Sunday Matters
Sunday Was God's Day—Now It Belongs to the NFL

As a society, we don't worship God much anymore—we worship entertainment. Now while I love entertainment, it cannot save or heal the human soul. It can only entertain and distract us from our own mind, our own heart, and our own life. Maybe that is why it is so popular. People are hurting and they want to feel better—and now even a distraction is better to them than to face their own dire need at a soul level.

Who would have thought that Hollywood's morality would be the thing to do? We admire celebrities so much that we follow their lead, and we see so many who can't keep a wife or a husband, and who exchange one person out for another, year after year, like relationships themselves do not matter. Is that advancing as a society? No. When the body is treated like it's trash—used and misused, bought and sold—and that becomes normal, is that advancing? When people don't even like who they are, is that advancing? No, it's not.

At one time Sunday was God's day—now it belongs to the NFL. I love football; I'm not against it! My team is the New Orleans Saints, and I love watching them play. But when I was young, football was played on Saturdays because Sunday was the Lord's day.

Church itself must fit a certain format for anybody to want to go—and it's as much fluff and as little truth as possible that fills the online pews. Still, people get up and live sick, disgusted, beat-up feeling lives of "barely getting by." They want sound bites, when God created their spirit to need a full buffet! Is that advancing? No it's not. We let our kids determine what church we go to or if we go at all. At one time your grandmother drug your butt to church—for your own good. Now, she lets you decide what's for your own good, and you aren't even grown enough to know! Is that advancing? No, it's not.

At one time the biggest buildings in town were the churches. Not anymore. You can't get people to a church on Sunday during football season in America. In 1967 you could buy a ticket to watch your team play for 6 bucks on a Saturday. Not today. You are going to pay—and you'll need to get there right during the time you should be feeding your spirit at church.

The not-so-funny part is that the NFL is non-profit, just like a church! Billions of dollars they don't pay taxes on because they are operating as if they are a church—and what morality are they bringing to society? And yet the atheists are trying to tear down churches and ministries, when it's the Church that brings the backbone of right living into society. You never hear them want to tear up the NFL's tax status. Why? Because they know that money is a power tool, and they are continually trying to break the power of the Church.

The Church itself needs money, but they don't want to talk about money. Churches will preach against your success and against your prosperity, and yet they still pass the bucket. They are embarrassed to preach a message that will encourage people to live godly lives of abundance—when the truth is that believers with more are believers who can do more. Abundant living is important.

When a believer advances spiritually, physically, and financially they can have an even greater affect on society—because they bring a more whole and full way of living into focus. They spend, but they aren't just spenders. They are givers! Abundant-minded believers are givers to society—and they do it on all sorts of levels. Of course, the devil wants to stop that. Of course, atheists don't want it. Abundant believers are a threat.

Sunday matters because spiritual education matters. At one time purchasing things was even slowed to a crawl on that day. Malls were closed on Sundays. Just about everything was closed on Sunday. You went to church and you ate with your family on Sunday—because it was a day of rest, a day for family, and ultimately a day we honored the Lord. Sunday mattered because it was a discipline of putting God and the family first, right at the beginning of the week.

Why Sunday Matters
Unrested People Make Bad Decisions

Not only is the spiritual teaching you get at Church important, but the social bonds you make are also important. It's necessary for human mental health and bodily health for us to be socially connected and create real relationships with others of like faith.

Sunday was once a day of rest—and a day of rest is critical for people. We need it. We are a stressed-out society. People want to continually be "connected" on a device, but are losing the will to be connected in real life with others. Many allow so many distractions to come in that they stop connecting with God as well.

Relationships in the Church matter, but they can't happen if nobody goes—and they can't happen if nobody stays to talk. You cannot have the same experience online as you do in person. Forget about being comfortable. Take your Sunday back! Your need to connect in real life and your need to spiritually feed your family is too important to let slide.

The wisdom you give your children is the wisdom they will pull on when life hits them with unexpected circumstances—do not set them up to fail by negating their spiritual education (Deuteronomy 11:19). I'm all for extracurricular activities, but the spiritual aspect of a person's life must also be attended to. Let it be a joy to teach your children the Word at home, and go to church, even if not every time you go to church is a joy. Do it as unto the Lord, and let your kids see your own discipline ruling your life.

Sunday matters because rest matters. When we took God's day and made it like every other day, not only did we remove the consistent and regular teachings we need to do life right, but we also gave up the basic physical need to take a true rest. Not rest from moving; but rest from the regular activities of the week.

We cannot live without pause. The Lord's Day gives us an opportunity to pause—to rest in Him and reflect on Him, and that gives our mind a break. It rejuvenates our spirit. We're here to live a good life and enjoy the life God gave us, and to help others. But it's hard to think about helping others and reaching the world with the Good News if we are not taking care of ourselves—and it is very hard to take care of yourself if you don't allow yourself that day to rest and reflect upon the Lord. Just like our body gets depleted, our spiritual reserves can get depleted.

Today, society is doggedly trying to live outside of God. But we only tax our mental and physical reserves when we try to live outside of God and do not take a day to rest before Him. God's order is good for the human mind, body, and spirit.

Without God, We Crumble from the Inside Out
Relationships Are Better When We Put God First

When we remove our Creator from our lives, and only live according to the ideas of our own mind and dictates of our own flesh, we set ourselves up for disaster. Without God, we crumble under the weight of a godless existence. Families are experiencing so much stress. Is that advancing? No. I see so many dads who aren't willing to take the responsibility of being a good father. I see so many women working themselves into the ground just trying to be both father and mother.

I see that our relationships aren't any better just because we're equal—and I believe in equality across the board, but the truth is that we've always been equal in value to God. Men and women are equal, but they are not the same—if we were the same, we'd understand each other a whole lot better! There would be very little divorce because we'd all agree all the time about everything. We don't. It's alright. We aren't supposed to think exactly the same way; we are not copies of each other. No matter how close we are, learning how to get along and overcome our differences is part of any good relationship.

Putting God first is important because without God at the forefront of our lives as individuals, we are depleted on a spiritual level. So, before we even start trying to give to somebody else, we are empty in the deepest kind of love. It's like trying to buy something with a credit card that's in the negative. The love that the Word teaches is not the love that society teaches. It is so much deeper and more profound, and if you learned an inkling of how to use it, you'd have a much better relationship not just with a spouse but with your children, your family, your coworkers, and even people on the street.

We've got to change because pride, selfishness, and a no-commitment mentality ruin what could be great relationships today. Marriage is commitment and it's hard to build a great one when you've got one foot out the door, ready to bolt whenever things get rough. I'm not against divorce; and I know there are times when it isn't just needful to divorce, but it's the best option given the circumstances. But the climate of divorce in this society is a "give up" and "give in" mentality.

Communicating Is Necessary—
The Principles of the Word Are Even More Necessary

We've got more information about communicating than any other generation before us, yet we can't get along? Communicating might be necessary but I believe the Word of God working in a person's life is even more necessary—because how can you build the best relationship if you aren't building the best you?

Two people working together can work it out, but to advance in any relationship, we must value commitment to that relationship (Proverbs 27:17). We must value commitment to God's principles. His principles shine a light on our gifts, talents, and inadequacies. God can purify your heart so that you can be your best self and shine for your loved one.

We must realize that no man or no woman can be a stand-in for Jesus. The best thing you can do for your marriage is work on yourself—spiritually and mentally—so that you bring the best you to the relationship. Otherwise, you're relating at whim and on whim, and let me tell you something, I've been married since 1970, to the same woman, (because you have to say that these days), and I've found out that commitment is a wonderful thing and worth working for.

The biggest work in a regular marriage isn't changing "them"; it's letting God change you. It's becoming the person God created you to be. It's treating your wife or husband to the best you instead of the worst you. In other words, it's bringing your "A game" home, and learning how to give mercy, love, and forgiveness when necessary.

Sometimes you just have to look them in the eye, say you're sorry, and ask for forgiveness—own what you did, show love, and start giving them your best self again. That's what my wife, Cathy, does and it works! (That was a little joke.)

Relationships don't have to be that much work. If you put the principles of God first in your own life, you will treat others

111

better—including those you love. Advancing in life is a lot more joyful when you have someone committed to being on your side for the ride.

Kids Need to Know More Than Algebra— Spiritual and Emotional Education Is Necessary, Too

We are so hard on our children today when it comes to accomplishing and succeeding in the world, yet we are so soft when it comes to teaching them anything spiritual. We've got an epidemic of children who are directionless and do not see anything wrong with being self-centered and entitled.

There is nothing wrong with the child—a child will act in accordance to what he or she has learned and will try to be acceptable. Today, they have more education but less teaching than ever! We push them to succeed, but we do not train them how to handle their thoughts.

Instead, we keep them so busy that they can't be kids anymore—and when they do have time with us, we give them screens to eat up their natural curiosity and energy. They are saying now that kids hide behind screens so much that they are losing the ability to interact well on a real-life level—the social graces are gone; and the respect for others that comes along with day-to-day interactions is going, too.

We need to teach our children how to handle conflict—because they don't seem to be learning much of that. They need to learn how to handle their emotions because, right now, it seems like many don't know what to do when someone's opinion is not like their own. They don't seem to know how to overcome. Outside of retaliation, many just don't seem to know what to do when they are angry, resentful, and frustrated. In other words, we aren't providing enough emotional or spiritual education—but they do know algebra!

We need God more than ever because we can't neglect the whole person. The Word is filled with teaching on how to properly condition the heart and mind in order to overcome conflict and obstacles in life. We have to step back and realize that the Word matters because people matter.

Our thought life is a huge part of us, and yet many children don't know what to do when thoughts about harming themselves or others come up in their mind. Many think every thought they have is their own, even though it's not. Many don't have any idea or concern about the realities of evil.

The reality of good and evil is taught in the Word of God—and no matter what people say, the reality of good and evil exists. Happiness is not found by letting the flesh run hog-wild. Peace is not found by ignoring evil in the world. The disconnected feeling is real in the lives of many, even though we've got more ways of connecting than ever before. People are living busy and disconnected lives, and their children are, too. And without God and spiritual instruction regarding what to do when the mind gets overloaded and the spirit feels empty, well...here we are.

People blame the guns—but guns have been around for a long time. It's the current mindset and lifestyle that is new. God is laughed at now. Even saying you are praying is looked down upon as if it is nothing. God as "the Answer" isn't even a thought, but we are raising a whole generation to be disassociated from the real needs of their own hearts. You can't divorce God from society, cut off most of your real relationships, and live in the near-constant virtual world of a screen and expect a great outcome.

What Is the Answer?
God Is the Answer

So, what is the answer? God is the Answer—and not as some far-off deity or a dictator of rules without reason. We must value our humanity, see our own potential, and recognize God, our Creator, as the best guide for life. We all have free will. Every single one of us is valuable to God and has a purpose worth knowing and living. It's about taking back God's day. It's about taking back the rest we get from that day, and the teaching we need to rise up and conquer the flesh that would destroy us if it remains unbridled.

The Church must rise up and be the example for what is good—not religion, but in matters of the human heart. Not just preachers, but believers—we all have a duty to the world to promote love, salvation, healing, and to encourage each other to live the good life God has given us.

We can rebuild our reputation and start being honorable every day in the eyes of our children and in the eyes of society. We can be examples to the world around us in how to advance, and change this mess in a generation. This book is about advancing because we need to advance spiritually, physically, and financially. Again, we are the examples for our children and society. They are not the examples for us.

God has given each of us a soul. Every person you see has one. And each is worth saving and loving—which means each is worth teaching and training how to live by the Spirit of God. As believers, we must show that we value others and care enough to put away distractions and refocus our own minds.

Humanity needs us to preach the Word of God as the moral benchmark for society at-large. They may not like it, but they need it—because right and wrong matter. Honor and dishonor matter. Life and death matter.

We help the world when we exercise God's principles in our own life and share them with others. We show the love of God to others when we share what we know in love. The inner work that we must do is sowing to the Spirit and building each other up in our like precious faith.

Love is demonstrative. It doesn't pick away at others; it lifts others up. Love teaches the truth; it can be confrontational, but it can still be loving. I sometimes say that love in its greatest form is discipline—and that means "correction" is love. It's not about beating someone down!

Correction is about helping others to see what is good so they don't fall into what is terrible in life. It's about the path of light and what's good; it is NOT a power struggle. We bring the light. We bring the wisdom. We bring the understanding. The Word is our guide and love is our way, and we are to be shining a light unto the path—because society needs more light so they can see the right path. Even if they choose not to go down it, they need to see it all lit up!

We do a disservice to our children and society at-large when we do not focus on Christ and the heart of His teachings in the Church—and when we do not live them in our personal lives. We cannot help others if we are too distracted or blasé to even help ourselves. The heart of the message is always the most important, and we help our children and all those they will one day influence when we teach it to them!

They will be the next generation. All these problems will be in their hands. Are they ready spiritually? Do they know God's ways at all? Or do they just know rules and regulations? The Word of God is training for the human spirit and mind—and it's for good, and not evil. It helps all of us to manage the mind God gave us, and helps us to overcome obstacles so we can advance in the life He gave us. How will they know if we don't share its truths?

God gave all of us a good purpose and a destiny of hope, including each of our children and everyone out there you see. The Church needs to share hope and truth in love. People need to be told what they can do and what they can have in life—and why living God's way is so good for the human heart. Without a vision for the future, people perish (Proverbs 29:18). Humanity was created for growth, for advancing....it's our job as the Church to help them do it.

Whatever You Do, Do It in Love

Love is energy and it should flow. Don't be somebody who clogs the pipes! As believers who make up the Church, we aren't here to crush spirits. We are here to lift spirits and promote God's message and all the subsequent goodness that comes from following God's Word.

God wants the best for all of us—so we should always want the best for others. Whether they are a child He places in our care or a person He puts on our path, it's our job to do everything in love. No passivity! Love!

A good rule of thumb is to remember the fruit of the Spirit (Galatians 5:22-23). Whatever portion of the Word you share with your children or anybody else, remember that as you teach it, it must be delivered in order to promote the attributes of God's Spirit. That means you can't teach love if you're angry and full of hate! You'll just mess it up. Pray each day that the Lord helps you to walk in His Spirit so that you can train others with the right spirit!

Love, joy, peace, patience, gentleness, goodness, faith, meekness, and self-control are what your words should promote—because all of these are what the human heart is capable of attaining, enjoying, and spreading throughout the world.

God is not separate from His Spirit. This means that if His Word is being taught outside of His attributes, it's not being taught right. The Word should never be used to promote hatred or division. It's meant to save, heal, deliver, and make things right—so the message itself must always be delivered with His Spirit in mind. Whether you share the Word or hear the Word, or both, just keep that in mind. It'll help you to stay on target as you share and as you hear others, it'll help you avoid those serpents masquerading as doves that mean you harm.

When the Spirit in the message is flowing, that's advancing! That's when the anointing knocks on the door of the heart. That's advancing! Because that's when people are reached and lives are changed for the better. That's when we get new brothers and sisters in the faith. Society is changed in the same way people are reached for the Lord—one soul at a time!

CHAPTER 13

We Need to Advance As the Church: "Frustrating" the Grace of God

God may look at the heart of man, but when it comes to everybody else? Well, they look at the outward appearance first! In other words, people notice you from the outside, not the inside.

Nobody sees what you "meant to do" or how you "wanted to be." You have to *show* them who you really are, and you are a vessel for Christ—and that means outward action. And because of that, you are a conduit for hope to those around you.

Advancing outwardly has always been part of the believer's life. But today there is a disappointing trend that, I believe, shows we aren't advancing. It's time to take it up a few notches! People need to see a difference between believers and non-believers—something more pure and joyful at the same time.

Today, purity seems to have gone out the window and the pollution of the world has not just taken ahold in the Church secretly, but it is outwardly manifesting just about everywhere I go.

Frustrating the Grace of God

Sin. Nobody talks about it anymore—but it's still a factor, and it's one that can cause you to stumble through life instead of succeeding in life. Advancing is about putting aside the things that act like weight on your shoulders. Your race is your life, and running it with God is easy unless you weigh yourself down with sin.

Jesus came to free you of every sin, and He did that on the cross. Nothing you can possibly do can separate you from the love of God (Romans 8:38-39). But there is plenty you can do to separate yourself from your own purpose and destiny. Don't give up your future. Refuse to be bent on self-destruction. You are free from the weight of sin the moment you accept Jesus as Lord. From that moment, and sometimes moment to moment, you begin living a life that is in your own best interest—you begin walking with God, learning from His Word, and enjoying the race.

It's in your own best interest to serve God and let sin go. It's not God trying to strong arm you into some box you can't fit into—it's you realizing that with God, you are always going to be your best self. You'll live a better life; the one your soul actually wants to live. You will become a better influence upon your family and even the world when you show up in an advancing state—spiritually, physically, emotionally, in your relationships, and yes, financially, too.

Sin is "missing the mark," and the Word tells us to "press toward the mark"—which means sin is going the opposite direction of God and of your own personal destiny. Hebrews 12:1 says, "...*let us lay aside every weight, and the sin which doth so easily beset us, and let us run with patience the race that is set before us.*"

Sin is obvious to your heart—it will weigh on your heart unless you do it so much that your conscience is seared as if by a hot iron. Even then, under the anointing of the Gospel, it will show up and you will feel the weight of it upon your soul. The human soul was not meant to live under the weight of sin.

Jesus came to wash away all that junk—but it's up to you to walk in your own victory and choose your own advancement by not going back to the sin He has delivered you from. The Word paints a vivid picture of that problem when it says, *"As a dog returneth to his vomit, so a fool returneth to his folly"* (Proverbs 26:11).

Grace Wasn't Given to Us to Help Us Sin Better

We are all saved by grace—but grace wasn't given to us by Jesus so that we could sin better. It was given so that we could overcome sin and run our race freely, without the distraction of sin's heavy weight upon the soul.

If you want to live by grace, live according to Galatians 2:20: *"I am crucified with Christ: nevertheless I live; yet not I, but Christ liveth in me: and the life which I now live in the flesh I live by the faith of the Son of God, Who loved me, and gave Himself for me."* That is not a life lived weighted by sin. That is a not a life that makes a mockery of the cross. That is not a life that uses the grace of God message as an excuse to live without self-control.

Galatians 2:21 makes that even clearer when it says, *"I do not frustrate the grace of God: for if righteousness come by the law, then Christ is dead in vain."* What does this mean? If you don't live by the *"faith of the Son of God,"* you are frustrating the grace of God.

Grace is not a Gospel. The Gospel is the birth, death, burial, resurrection, and ascension of the Lord Jesus Christ. Grace is a doctrine, and I believe in it—but it should make you want to sin less, not more!

I literally heard a man once say that if you are watching pornography, just say to yourself, "I am the righteousness of God." Listen, you can tell yourself anything you want to, but the truth is non-negotiable. If pornography isn't wrong to you, why do you cut if off if your wife or your kids come in the room? If gossiping isn't wrong, why do you whisper or stop talking if the person comes in the room? If whatever you are doing isn't wrong, why do you need to hide it or do it in the dark, and ultimately, why does your very soul know it's not good?

You are saved by grace—and I don't care if you sinned five minutes ago, you can be washed clean of it by simply turning to God and asking for forgiveness. Any teaching that negates your need to turn to God is not in your best interest to accept into your life. You need to turn to God. Before you were saved, you needed God. After you are saved, you still need God. You will be pulling on that cleansing blood all of your life—but as a believer, your goal should be to pull on it less and less, until you barely ever need to ask forgiveness from God at all.

Do not deliberately frustrate the good grace of your God. The sin you want to do may feel good for a moment, but it's not worth it—it's a weight on your back keeping you from advancing. Lay it aside. Put it away. Tell it where to go.

Recognize the Presence of God

Start making it a point to recognize the presence of God in your everyday life. He sees it all and is with you—He's in the room with you because He's inside of you. Remind yourself that there is a spiritual world you cannot yet see, but one day you will see it clearly. Nothing is really hidden.

Advancing outwardly means you've made a commitment to run your race with purity and without fear—because you know that God is with you, and Christ has redeemed you, and God wants the best for you. Of course, God will forgive you for anything. But to advance in life, you must accept that forgiveness, which means you have to forgive yourself, too. Some of the most hate-filled people are those who cannot forgive themselves. The more mercy you receive from God, the more merciful you should be to yourself and to others.

When you refuse to carry the weight of sin, you will run with much more freedom. Others love to see people who are truly free inside. We celebrate those who have overcome. They are inspiring. It's success from the inside out and for the believer, this kind of advancement is born out of faith in God.

Purity Opens Your Eyes

It's easier to see what is of God in your daily life when you work on being pure of heart. As Jesus taught in the beatitudes, the pure in heart are the ones that shall "see" God (Matthew 5:8). I like to think of it like this: Purity opens your eyes!

It just becomes easier to detect what's not pure if your eyes are focused on what is pure. This means it's a lot easier to avoid temptation because the stumbling blocks stand out to you like blinking lights. The purity inside of you taps your spirit, and you just know that whatever it is that's not pure isn't of God—which just means it isn't for you. If it's not good, it isn't for you! It won't advance the plan God has for your life.

You might think that purity is "outside" of you somewhere, but it's not. It's inside of you. All you have to do is focus on it and let it come out. This is about sowing to the spirit. If you struggle, it's time to make a decision to stop giving the problem so much credit and so much power! Turn the tables on yourself and make purity the focus instead.

If you focus on the problem, you just give more attention and energy to what you want out of your life. If you focus on the solution and that solution is the purity of God, the purity you want to manifest in your life will push out the pollution of the world that is trying to run your life.

You are in the power seat because you have God inside of you. There is nothing you can't beat. Focusing on the solution is how you let go of the problem. It's how you slough off what you don't want so that you can run the race God has set before YOU—and win!

Step-by-Step—Nobody Runs a Race Any Other Way

People always remember winners. The names of losers are rarely written in books and never inscribed on trophies. Why? Because people gravitate to victory. God created us with a craving for it, both in ourselves and in watching others achieve it. But it will be very difficult for you to advance if you are still carrying around extra baggage—so unload that junk and advance outwardly. There are people you need to reach for God.

You are a beautiful example of what freedom really looks like. If you struggle, start saying that about yourself. Don't identify with that baggage anymore. Your freedom in God is worth the effort of speaking by faith with confidence, and raising your opinion of yourself. In Christ, you can do all things because He gives you the strength to do it. Talk to yourself and claim your heritage of strength. That baggage isn't yours. Because Christ is in you, it's not even hard—it's easy. Aim for purity and speak confidently *about* yourself *to* yourself!

Sometimes we look at people who are free in God and think they were always that way—but the truth is that they've learned how to rely upon the Lord and conquer what once so easily beset them. And they've done it step-by-step because nobody runs a race any other way. They've learned how to run their race without hurting themselves anymore. They've learned how to soar and succeed in manifesting what they want.

I love seeing those who are advancing outwardly because I know that they didn't get there without advancing inwardly, too. Their testimonies are a blessing, and their freedom in God is admirable. They are examples of what God can do in our life when we realize we are hooked up to Him in spirit and truth.

That kind of freedom not only brings glory to God, but it is a magnet for others who are struggling and need that same freedom. It gives us an opportunity to share what we've learned, and to help others let go of the weights and start running free again.

Remember, you are meant to live free and light—to run your race *with* grace. Don't frustrate the grace of God. Aim higher! Go for purity of heart because you need it to feel light, and the world needs that, too. Grace, in its truest manner, sets its affection on things above and not on things below. Grace, in its truest manner, makes the choice to live better, not worse, by looking up!

Why not show the world a Christian athlete that knows how to conquer and throw out the baggage that causes so many to stumble and live so low? Why not show them how to be free by looking up? Don't keep the Christ in you hidden. Your light is too valuable to hide. Let go of the baggage and focus on the purity within you, through Christ Jesus, so you can *continue* in freedom and be blessed.

I believe that James 1:25 says it best: *"But whoso looketh into the perfect law of liberty, and continueth therein, he being not a forgetful hearer, but a doer of the work, this man shall be blessed in his deed."* Freedom is your birthright in Christ, and whatever you do is more blessed when you do it out of your free place. So, don't let anything hold you back. You were always meant to be a winner going somewhere to win—you were always meant to be free in Jesus.

CHAPTER 14

Anything Worth Having or Doing Is Worth the Effort of "Pressing Toward the Mark"

Is there effort in advancing? Yes! Is it worth it? Yes! Anything worth having or doing is worth the effort of "pressing toward the mark." You will not value what you do not put an effort toward gaining, even if that effort is simply walking by faith and not by sight. Even if that effort is just speaking the Word, drawing in what you want, and living praising His name. The prize of reaching your goal is so valuable, but the journey of who you are going to become in the process is invaluable.

As you can tell by reading this book, advancing in any way as a believer always begins by putting God first—He's Alpha and Omega, the Author and Finisher of your faith. To make Him and His way of doing things the center of your life is what I call advancing upwardly.

Advancing upwardly isn't just thinking about Heaven, the place. No, it's about creating a little bit of Heaven's way of doing things right here on earth—in your thoughts, in your words, and in your actions. Faith in God is everything. Trusting the God Who trusts in you is key, too.

I know that pressing toward the mark isn't always easy—if it was easy, everybody would do it. Just the words *"pressing toward"* reveal that what is ahead of you will take effort. But it's not impossible, and with faith it's not even going to be hard. It just takes doing. It takes living. Most importantly, it takes recognizing God's abundant nature living in you—He must be the foundation of all your dreaming, all your doing, and all your achieving in life. Everything you manifest by faith comes out of His great limitless Being.

This is why I believe that we advance in every good way when we follow the verse that says, *"Set your affection on things above, not on things on the earth"* (Colossians 3:2). I want you to notice that it doesn't say we are supposed to abandon the things of the earth. God wouldn't have put us right here on earth if all He wanted us to do was think about being somewhere else, even if it is Heaven! The Word is giving us a valuable lesson in this short verse—it's talking about affection, which is a demonstration of love, care, and concern.

What Does *"Affection"* for *"Things Above"* Mean?

What are the *"things above"*? How do we demonstrate *"affection"* for them? I'm going to tell you this: The "things above" are the attributes of God's Spirit; the way that heavenly people interact. The things up there run a lot smoother than down here for a reason— everybody is walking in the light of God. Everybody has advanced upwardly as far as they can go!

Imagine if Heaven came to earth...how would you act then? That's advancing upwardly. The way they do things above is the way we should start doing them below, and our affection should be for Heaven's ways of acting in the world.

The good ways that come out of God's Spirit and rest in ours, those are what our affection should be upon. Those good things are what we are here to advance. It's our job to flood this world with the fruit of the Spirit—to put more of what's "up there" down here in this dark, dark world.

You aren't here just to live for yourself. God has put things in you that the world needs—and it's time to start seeing them within yourself as valuable to humanity. These are the areas within you that you can easily access. They need to be spread around because people need the spirit of God in action, in demonstration, from a place of affection—from YOU.

Advancing upwardly is about living God's way, every day—to the very best of your ability as you put your faith in Him to help you do it. Yes, you can still see all your personal visions, dreams, and goals come to pass. In fact, you'll probably see them come a lot sooner because when you advance upwardly, the energy of God pulsates through actions that demonstrate His Spirit. When His Spirit flows through us strongly and we aim our faith, manifestations show up quicker—and we do it while blessing humanity at the very same time. It's amazing how quickly God can do things when we start working with Him instead of against Him.

What Does It Look Like in Practical Terms?

So, what does advancing upwardly look like in practical terms? It looks like generosity—like giving to those in need and blessing those who don't need a thing! It looks like tangibly helping others when they need it—being compassionate as you walk through life and noticing when it's your time and your turn to reach out and be the blessing to someone else.

It looks like pure kindness—like walking through life with the express purpose of giving respect and honor to others simply because they are human and made in God's image. There is no person on this planet that is hopeless, though many are told that they are.

Again, advancing upwardly is showing affection (love, care, and concern) for the things above, and that means doing what they do "above"—except doing it down here, where it's needed most. We are God's hands extended. I hope you advance upwardly and let God use you in this way because, as I so often say, "The only Jesus some people may ever see is the Jesus in you or the Jesus in me." We have been called to advance upwardly.

"I press toward the mark for the prize of the high calling of God in Christ Jesus" is rarely more enjoyable and valuable than when we do it in a giving-state toward others. To *"press toward the mark"* in this way is to live continually aware of giving and receiving—it becomes a practical discipline. We start where we are. We continue as we move through life toward the personal dreams we have. But every day is an opportunity to give and receive.

Do you have the joy of the Lord in abundance? Give it away. Let joy be like seeds you sow everywhere you go. God will pour more joy into you as you do! You will feel wonderful as you advance upwardly in this way—spreading the joy of the Lord and giving affection to others is definitely from way up above!

Are you easily a peacemaker? Do you notice how much strife is in the world, maybe in your family, or among friends? If you are a peacemaker, and I hope you are, then it's your job to make peace wherever you go. Jesus did not call us to "keep" peace, He called us to "make" peace. Consider this a seed because it is! And God will not only reward you, but you will see incredible change in the world around you as you do it.

Are you a confident believer? Then you have a seed to give— because this world is full of people who do not know their value or worth, and are fearful to believe in themselves. If you are confident in God, then you have a job to spread that to others. Imagine the lives you could change if you only spoke up and encouraged those who needed it as they came along your path?

Are you full of wisdom? Then you have a wealth of seeds in you to sow into the lives of others—consider the youth and the young, but also consider how you might bring that wisdom out at small moments in your everyday life. If you want to advance upwardly and bring the wisdom of life that is found in God into the world, set your affection on that heavenly thing!

Wisdom and understanding are desperately needed in the world today. Don't wait for somebody to call you out and use you that way—just start dispersing a little everywhere you go. I promise you that you don't need a stadium of people hearing you to make a difference. You have no idea the depths to which God can and will use you if you will only reach out.

We also need to be aware of how much we are receiving, too—because one of the worst problems I see with people in the world today is a lack of gratitude and appreciation. They often seem to be scrambling for something more, without even saying thank you to God or to each other for what they have already.

We have received so much—our heart should always be appreciative to God for all His many blessings and for what He's done. Whether it's spiritual, physical, financial, or in our relationships with others, we should always remember the good that we have—and thank God for it. The more we spread appreciation, the better our families will be, our children will be, our church will be, and our world will be! There is very little that will raise your spirits more than realizing what you have to be grateful for right now—and you can do that as you are believing for much bigger, better, and more.

You see, the lie of the devil is that you can't have it all. That you must choose. No, there is no lack in Heaven, as you've just read in this book—and you don't have to choose or settle. There is goodness in God, and there's enough for ALL.

Unity—It's God's Heart for the Church

One of the saddest things going on in the world today is the rampant strife between people—strife is something God says that He hates. Strife is like cancer in the body of Christ, but it is ravaging humanity at an even greater pace. As believers, when we advance upwardly, we stop strife in its tracks. We shut down disharmony. We are promoters of unity. Not unity of doctrine, but unity of the faith.

"Unity of the faith" is not the same thing as "unity of doctrine." Nowhere does it say we ALL have to believe exactly the same. Nowhere does it say we should all be Catholics, Baptists, Methodists, Episcopalians, Anglicans, or whatever group in the Christian faith you might belong to. All God is interested in when it comes to religion is "the unity of the faith."

So, what is "the faith"? It's simply Jesus Christ, the hope of Glory—the Lamb slain before the foundation of the world, sent to redeem mankind, and give each of us a way to the Father. It's the message of how, *"For God so loved the world, that He gave His only begotten Son, that whosoever believeth in Him should not perish, but have everlasting life"* (John 3:16).

If we can agree on John 3:16, we are unified in faith. The world needs to see the Church unified. If we can't get along with each other, what kind of message are we sending to the world? We serve the Prince of Peace—not the Duke It Out of Doubt!

There is healing to be done in the Church because we have a strife-filled past, but that healing doesn't have to take long. In fact, it starts the moment we ask for forgiveness and just start flowing in God's Spirit of love. It's as simple as a choice. It takes just a moment, and everything from that moment on can begin to change.

Heaven Is Family...Without the Family Problems!

I love being a believer. I love being in the family of God. We have some problems, who doesn't? But can we press toward the mark and bust through them with love and faith? Yeah, we can! We're going to make it, all the way to Heaven. You know, if you just think about the nature of Heaven, it's really just about family...but without the "family problems"!

As you advance in your life, I hope you'll never forget that we are here with a purpose—not just to fulfill our own dreams and goals, but to bring heavenly ways right down here to earth. Jesus prayed for His Father's will to be done here on earth as it is in Heaven, and if you learn nothing else from this book, I hope you will take that away and go out and start doing it.

I hope this book has blessed you as much as the revelation blessed me when God put it on my heart. I pray that it becomes a revelation to you, too—one that brings inspiration and manifestation into your own life.

God has so much for you. You can do whatever is in your heart and have whatever is good in this life—if you are willing to "press toward the mark" and see advancing as God's will for you. What you do matters—not just to you, but to your family and friends, and to your community as well as the Church...ultimately, it matters to God's vision for the world.

I don't know about you, but I didn't give my heart to God in order to live a mediocre life—and since I've been "pressing toward the mark" it's been anything but boring! The believer's life is an adventure and a true journey of faith.

In closing, I challenge you to really run your race. Run it with faith and joy. Run it with love. One day we'll all be together in Heaven, but for now we've got things to do right here on earth! God has you here for a reason, and that reason is to advance. So, what are you going to do? Where are you going to go? What are you going to have? Don't be afraid to live your best life—the one that is in your heart.

You are going to go to bed tonight and wake up tomorrow anyway. Why not wake up ready to really "press toward the mark" in life? Just imagine where God will take you if you do?! Just imagine how much Heaven you can create right here on earth?! Don't worry about "how" you're going to do everything. Just concentrate on having faith in God today. Right here, right now, it's time to forget those things that are behind you and move forward to what lies ahead. So, shake off the cobwebs, man! Take a deep breath and stretch, too. Today is the day. There is just no better time than now to ADVANCE!

Prayer of Salvation

"For God so loved the world, that He gave His only begotten Son, that whosoever believeth in Him should not perish, but have everlasting life. For God sent not His Son into the world to condemn the world; but that the world through Him might be saved."

John 3:16-17

God loves the world. He sent His Son, Jesus, to make a way for all of us to be free—from guilt, from shame, and from every sin and misstep no matter how big or small. Salvation removes the heavy chains of sin and a life lived apart from our Maker. Christ's death and resurrection on the cross was sacrificial—He did it for you and me, and for the whole world so that we could have that blank slate and simply start again.

Accepting God's plan of salvation through Jesus Christ is the first step to living at the top because, as Mark 8:36 says, *"For what shall it profit a man, if he shall gain the whole world, and lose his own soul?"* Nothing is as important as being right with God in your heart, and by accepting Christ, you are doing just that.

If you don't know Jesus today, if you've never prayed a prayer of salvation, or if you just need to come back home to God where you belong, would you take a moment and pray with me today? This prayer below is a guide. Feel free to talk from your heart. Wherever you are right now, no matter what your situation, God will meet you where you are—He will hear your prayer, loose the chains of bondage off your soul, and set you free with the blood of His precious Son, Jesus. Pray with me now:

"God, thank You for loving me enough to send Your Son. I know that I need You. I believe that You are my God, my Maker, and my Father—and I believe that You sent Your only begotten Son to die for me. I believe that He died and rose again for me, too, so that I could be washed clean of all my sins. Jesus, come into my life right now. Wash me clean and create a new heart in me now. Thank You for paying the price for me. From this point on, I will seek to serve You and love You, and I ask You to help me to find my destiny in You—to be whole in every area of my life. May Your blessings follow me all the days of my life as I learn from You. Thank You, Jesus, for saving me! My new life starts right now, Lord. This is my God-day, and I'm never turning back!"

If you have prayed this prayer or if this book has helped you to create a good life in Christ, would you write and let me know? Please write to:

Jesse Duplantis Ministries
P.O. Box 1089
Destrehan, LA 70047-1089
www.jdm.org

About the Author

Jesse Duplantis is what some would call a true evangelist. Supernaturally saved and delivered from a life of addiction in 1974 and called by God to the office of evangelist in 1978, he founded Jesse Duplantis Ministries with the sole mission of world evangelism at whatever the cost. And he has continuously done that for four decades of ministry work.

With a television ministry that spans the globe and a preaching itinerary that has taken him to thousands of different churches to date, Jesse is still fulfilling his original call to evangelism with gusto! His commitment to Christ, long-standing integrity in ministry, and infectious, joyful nature have made him one of the most loved and respected ministers of the Gospel today.

Often call the "Apostle of Joy" because of his hilarious illustrations, Jesse's anointed preaching and down-to-earth style has helped to open the door for countless numbers of people to receive Jesus as their Lord and Savior. Jesse has proven through his own life that no matter who you are or where you come from, God can change your heart, develop your character through His Word, and help you find and complete your divine destiny.

To contact Jesse Duplantis Ministries,
write or call:

Jesse Duplantis Ministries
P.O. Box 1089
Destrehan, LA 70047-1089
www.jdm.org

Please include your prayer requests
and comments when you write.